WINSTON CHURCHILL

The Contradictions of Greatness

Churchill

The Contradictions of Greatness

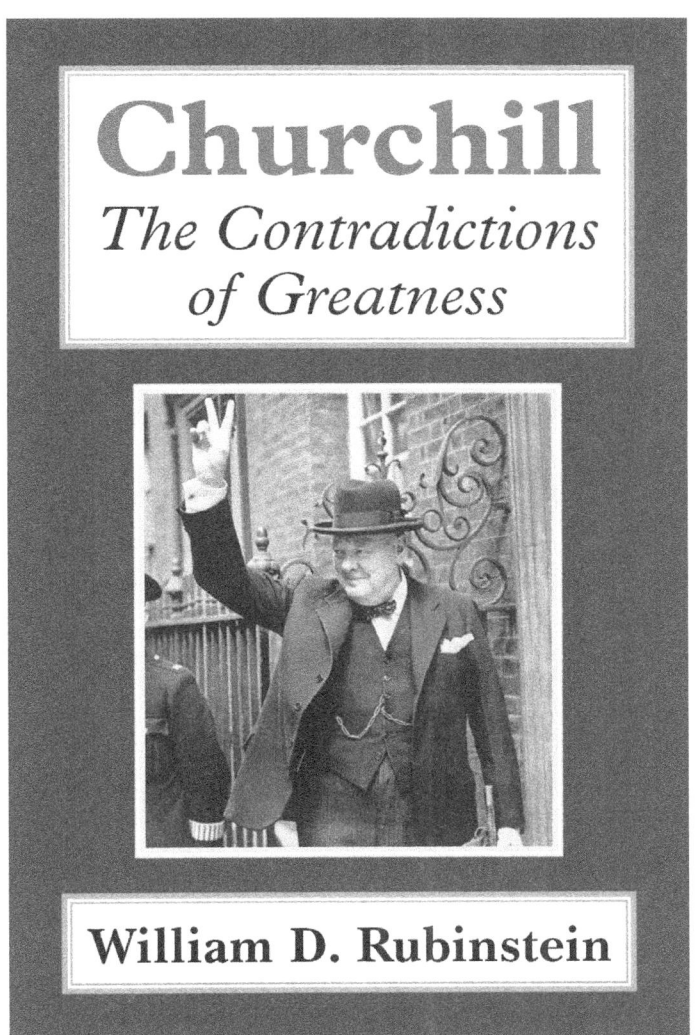

William D. Rubinstein

EER
Edward Everett Root, Publishers, Brighton, 2020.

EER

Edward Everett Root, Publishers, Co. Ltd.,
30 New Road, Brighton, Sussex, BN1 1BN, England.
www.eerpublishing.com

Details of our overseas agents are given on our website.

edwardeverettroot@yahoo.co.uk

William D. Rubinstein
Winston Churchill. The Contradictions of Greatness

© William D. Rubinstein 2020.

First published in England 2020.

This edition © Edward Everett Root Publishers, 2020.

ISBN: 9781912224227 (Hardback)
ISBN: 9781912224234 (eBook)

Cover and book production by Pageset Ltd, High Wycombe, Buckinghamshire.

Contents

The Author vii

Introduction ix

1. Winston Churchill and Tariff Reform 1
2. Churchill and Bolshevism 53
3. Winston Churchill and The Nazis 79
4. Churchill and the Jews 105
5. Churchill, The Empire and The United
   States 129

Churchill – Anomalies of Greatness –
   Bibliography 143
Churchill – Anomalies of Greatness – Index . . . 147

THE AUTHOR

WILLIAM D. RUBINSTEIN IS A LEADING AND widely published historian. He was Professor of History at the University of Aberystwyth 1995–2011. He is now an adjunct professor at Monash University in Melbourne, Australia. He was previously Professor of Social and Economic History at Deakin University in Victoria, Australia. He is a Fellow of the Australian Academy of the Humanities, of the Australian Academy of the Social Sciences, and of the Royal Historical Society. His major series of works are now published by *EER:*

Who Were The Rich? 4 volumes covering 1809–1859 now available. Volumes covering 1860–1914 to follow.

Men Of Property. The Very Wealthy In Britain Since The Industrial Revolution.

Unsolved Historical Mysteries. Answers To Outstanding Historical Puzzles.

Elites and the Wealthy In Modern British History.

Beyond the Dreams of Avarice. The Very Wealthy in Modern Britain.

Introduction

ALTHOUGH COUNTLESS WORKS HAVE BEEN written on Winston Churchill, few if any have come to grips with the many anomalies and curious features among the positions he took throughout his enormously long career. Churchill's political life is littered with strange and unaccountable stances he took on a wide variety of controversial matters. Historians have seldom highlighted or discussed these as anomalies, often preferring to see his career as a seamless web leading inevitably to his 'Finest Hour' in 1940, Britain's greatest modern Statesman, who was always right. Churchill was almost certainly

Britain's greatest modern Statesman, who was 'right' remarkably often, but it is the thesis of this book that he often took strange and virtually unaccountable stances throughout his life, whose anomalousness have been misunderstood by contemporary observers and many later historians. Churchill was both a very complex figure, whose unusual stances are often not easy fully to understand but also a rather simple one whose underlying worldview arguably revolved at almost all times around his belief in the hegemony of the English-speaking peoples and in a fundamental and permanent alliance between Britain and America.

This work examines a number of Churchill's anomalous positions. It begins with a discussion of his very curious stance on 'Tariff Reform' in the first decade of the twentieth century, an issue which does not appear to have been directly discussed by previous historians. It then looks at his reaction to Bolshevism and the November 1917 Russian Revolution and to the rise of Nazism. This is followed by discussions of Churchill's stance on the Jews and

Zionism, and on Churchill, the British Empire, and the Anglo-American Alliance. All of these positions were, it is argued, unusual and could not necessarily be predicted by Churchill's previous career. It is a measure of Churchill's greatness that he remains elusive and sometimes difficult to understand, in spite of all the millions of words written about him. But the underlying consistency is there, and Churchill's views and courage saved Britain and Western democracy.

Chapter One

WINSTON CHURCHILL AND TARIFF REFORM

A GOOD DEAL OF EXPLANATION MUST BE given for beginning this book with a chapter on Winston Churchill and Tariff Reform, a topic about which few besides specialist historians know very much, or, indeed, have ever heard. Yet the topic is both intrinsically important in understanding key aspects of Churchill's career, especially in its early phases, and in and of itself. More significantly,

Churchill's attitude towards Tariff Reform can be seen as an archetype for the main theme of this book that he frequently took unaccountable stances on a variety of key issues, stances which regularly, but not invariably, proved to be brilliantly justified.

'Tariff Reform' is the name given to the proposals by Joseph Chamberlain in 1903 to enact a tariff barrier around the whole British Empire. It was a revolutionary suggestion. Since the early nineteenth century Britain had systematically and deliberately reduced all of its tariff barriers, most famously with the repeal of the Corn Laws in 1846, in order to enact 'free trade', a economy in which any imported goods could enter the United Kingdom without paying a duty or tariff. Belief in Free Trade became the backbone of nineteenth-century British Liberalism and of the Liberal Party, and was also accepted, perhaps most reluctantly, by the Conservatives. Free Trade allowed British manufacturers to import raw material at the cheapest price; and similarly allowed British consumers to import foods and finished goods at the lowest price and from the widest international range. It allegedly raised living standards by reducing production costs to the manufacturer and the cost of living to the consumer, especially working class consumers. In an age before either much state control of the economy or any knowledge of macroeconomics and Keynesianism, it was one of the few means whereby the state could attempt to raise living standards or improve the economy. Free Trade was often linked with the mid-Victorian Liberal programme of 'peace, retrenchment, and reform', the paring back of state expenditures and the elimination of 'Old Corruption' and direct government expenditures on the rich and the aristocracy. Free Trade was widely seen as one of the main reasons why Britain became the 'workshop of the world' and why Europe escaped any general wars between 1815 and 1914. It is difficult to overstate the importance of Free Trade in the ideology of Victorian liberalism, and belief in it has often been compared to a religion.

Free Trade remained unchallenged until the 18809s at the earliest. From the 1880s however,

Britain's economic and industrial hegemony were increasingly challenged by the new, rising powers of Germany and the United States, as well as by other European states and Japan. What most of these states had in common, and especially Germany and the United States, is that they prospered behind high tariff walls. The deliberate use of tariffs to spur industrial development became one of the backbones of Bismarckian Germany, and – as is now forgotten – for decades it was *the* defining stance which separated the Republican and Democratic parties in the United States. The Republican party of Abraham Lincoln and his successors, building on the similar programmes of the earlier Federalist and American Whig parties, centrally advocated a high tariff barrier to allow America to develop large-scale world class industries, while the Democrats traditionally favoured low tariffs. Even within the British Empire, Free Trade was increasingly challenged. In Australia, Victoria, with its industrial centre of Melbourne, enacted tariffs while South Wales remained truer to Free Trade. (Australia consisted of separate self-governing colonies until

Federation in 1901.)

High tariff walls in Germany and America meant that German and American goods could be imported freely into Britain, while British goods had to pay a tariff to be allowed into America or Germany, set at a rate which often effectively excluded them. In particular, it was argued, foreign tariffs penalised British manufactured goods and British agricultural exports, and gave an obviously unfair advantage to the British economy. By the late Victorian period, these criticisms were more than theoretical: Britain was rapidly losing its economic superiority precisely to Germany and the United States, and especially in cutting-edge manufactured goods. From about 1880, too, Britain experienced a deep agricultural depression as frozen meats and other foodstuffs were imported freely from America, Australia, Argentina, and elsewhere. By the late Victorian period, Free Trade was increasingly challenged, and what was called the 'Fair Trade' movement arose in the 1880s which demanded retaliation against foreign countries which put tariffs on British exports. The

'Fair Trade' movement did not yet have mainstream political support in Britain. One of its few tentative supporters in the late nineteenth century, ironically, was Lord Randolph Churchill, Winston's father. Free Trade still enjoyed mainstream support, including the support of virtually everyone in the Liberal party and from most economists. They pointed out that the imposition of tariffs by Germany and America merely meant that their citizens would have to pay more for imported goods than Englishmen, and had a narrower choice of goods. Tariffs were applied because of lobbying by venal interest groups, especially in America, and brought corruption in their wake. Britain also continued to benefit as the 'clearing house of the world', with the City of London as the world's financial hub and British ships carrying most of the world's trade, both of which would be injured by the imposition of British tariffs.

This situation continued until 1903. On 15 May1903, Joseph Chamberlain (1836–1914) made what was one of the most important, sensational, and momentous speeches of its time. Although remembered today only by historians, with the possible exception of Lloyd George's vituperative Limehouse speech of July 1909, it was probably the most famous and significant speech made by a British public figure in the quarter-century before the outbreak of the First World War. Chamberlain's place in British political life was arguably unique, then or since. He was, famously, a Unitarian screw manufacturer in Birmingham (although he was born in London and educated at University College School) who began his political career as the leader of Birmingham's municipal radicals who introduced 'municipal socialism' and extensive public works into that city. After election to Parliament as a radical Liberal in 1876, in 1886 he broke decisively with Gladstone and Irish Home Rule, becoming one of the leaders of the Liberal Unionist Party which was increasingly an open associate of the Tories. In 1895 he was included in Lord Salisbury's mainly Conservative Cabinet, and chose to become Colonial Secretary rather than some higher office. Between 1899 and 1902 he is widely seen as the main architect of the Boer War, which, after many travails, brought the Boer Republic into the British Empire. Chamberlain increasingly saw the unity of the British Empire as his main political aim and goal. In 1902–03 Chamberlain went on an extensive tour of the Empire. He had already attempted to get the British Cabinet to introduce some form of tariff policy which would, while excluding foreign goods, give preference to foodstuffs, raw materials, and manufactured goods produced in the Empire. His great Birmingham speech of May 1903 decisively threw down the gauntlet, rejecting the principles of the 'small remnants of Little Englanders of the Manchester School' but instead introduce 'if necessary, retaliation' in the form of tariffs when British or colonial interests were threatened. (Cited in Richard Jay, *Joseph Chamberlain: A Political Study* (Oxford, 1981), p.272.)

The first point which might be made about Chamberlain's speech is that there is almost certainly no equivalent in modern British politics of a middle-ranking Cabinet minister suggested a fundamental and far-reaching change in British policy without consulting his colleagues or securing the permission of the Prime Minister or the Cabinet (which Chamberlain did not ask for or receive). Perhaps no one except Chamberlain would have done such a thing, and it is rather remarkably that he was not sacked from the Cabinet on the spot. (A somewhat similar case occurred in 1968 when Enoch Powell, a member of Edward Heath's Shadow Cabinet, made his famous 'rivers of blood' anti-immigrant speech; Powell was immediately sacked from the Shadow Cabinet by Heath.)

Even more significant were the range of responses to Chamberlain's May 1903 speech. For some Tariff Reform (as Chamberlain's movement came to be known) activists, his speech was, literally, the decisive movement of their political lives. Leopold Amery (1873–1955), in an oft-quoted remark, called Chamberlain's 'challenge ... as direct and provocative as the theses which Luther nailed to the church door at Wittenberg'. (Cited in Richard Jay, *Joseph Chamberlain: A Political Study*

(Oxford,1981), pp.271–272.) Amery, a First from Balliol and a Fellow of All Souls, had originally been a Fabian socialist, and then a member of Lord Milner's 'kindergarten' I South Africa. As a result of Chamberlain's Tariff Reform proposals, Amery became perhaps its keenest intellectual proponent, serving in Parliament from 1911 till 1945 and in the Cabinet for nearly twelve years as a lifelong Tariff Reformer and advocate of Imperial Preference (as Chamberlain's programme was also known), until his death more than half a century later. Another long-time activist was Henry Page Croft (1881–1942, later Sir Henry and then Lord Croft), who was non-political until 1903. 'The Chamberlain idea … appealed to me as something really constructive and the most attractive of his proposals was the idea of Imperial Reference which I hoped and believed might lead to an Imperial Zollverein and possibly ultimate federation. I leapt into the fray and immediately started an organisation of the Tariff Reform League in East Herts.' (Lord Croft, *My Life of Strife* (London, n.d. [1947]), p.41. The 'Zolverein' was the German customs union, designed to eliminate tariffs among the German states, founded in 1818 which led to eventual German unification in 1871. The Tariff Reform League was the body founded by Chamberlain to advance his ideas.) Like Amery, Croft remained a lifelong Tariff Reformer, serving in Parliament from 1910 until he was made a peer in 1940 and was an important figure on the right wing of the Tory party. In 1908 a young Canadian businessman, Max Aitken (1879–1964), came to England in large part to further the cause of imperial unity and Tariff Reform. He made contact with Page Croft, and through him was adopted as a Conservative parliamentary candidate (Croft, *Ibid.*, p.78). Although wealthy, he did not yet own any newspapers, although by 1916 he both acquired the *Daily Express* and received a peerage, becoming Lord Beaverbrook. Beaverbrook also remained a lifelong advocate of Chamberlain's ideas until he died many decades later. Many other converts to Tariff Reform emerged almost immediately, sweeping most – but not all – Conservative M.P.s, peers, activists and intellectuals with it.

Chamberlain had the opposite effect on the Liberal party. Disunited and dispirited, and out of office since 1895, Chamberlain's programme helped to unify the Liberal party, and was one of the most important reasons for its sweeping electoral victory in 1906. All Liberals rejected Tariff Reform, all regarding Free Trade as sacrosanct. They believed that tariffs could only harm those who imposed them, and denied that their imposition would benefit Britain's economy or decrease unemployment. Opposition to tariffs was a feature throughout the Liberal party, even among the so-called Liberal Imperialists such as H.H. Asquith, Sir Edward Grey, and Richard Haldane who fully accepted the value of the Empire.

Chamberlain's programme had several independent but closely associated ends. Chamberlain and most of his strong supporters believed that the Twentieth Century would be the century of large nations and Empires, and that only the largest nations or Empires could remain as Great Powers, with smaller nations inevitably falling behind. There were several large nations which seemed assured of Great Power status in the twentieth century: the United States, of course; and probably Russia if it modernised and did not disintegrate. Germany would also be a Great Power, especially if it could unify the German-speaking areas of central Europe and extend its authority elsewhere. Britain was much more problematical: as an economic power it had seemingly passed its peak. But it could remain a Great Power if it succeeded in unifying its vast Empire, which included one-fourth of the world's population and had at least a pretence on every continent. This, however, was intrinsically difficult, given the centrifugal factors working against unity, especially the perceived national interests of the semi-independent white Dominions such as Canada and Australia. (The question which seems most pertinent to us, whether India and Africa could remain in the Empire in the long run, was hardly asked at the time.) For imperial unity realistically to be furthered, Chamberlain reasoned, wide-ranging measures would have to be introduced which unified the Empire economically, enabling it to function as a single unit with many parts. Chamberlain's scheme thus always envisioned a tariff around the whole Empire, not just Britain, which would impose restrictions on foreign goods but would give preference to all parts of the Empire. Only this, reasoned Chamberlain, and his supporters, could save the British Empire from inevitable collapse and disintegration, and preserve it as a Great Power in the twentieth century.

Chamberlain's scheme had other aims as well. Chamberlain was an advocate of social reform and of the introduction of measures which would initiate a British Welfare State, such as unemployment insurance and old age pensions. These were inevitable, as well as justified in their own right. But they would have to be paid for. Liberals and the left generally increasingly favoured paying for such measures by higher direct taxation on high incomes, especially on high landed incomes. ('Higher' taxation was relative: in 1910, after the Liberal government had been in office for over four years, someone earning £10,000 a year – the equivalent of around £700,000 today – paid only about £750 in income tax, less than 8 per cent of his income.) Tories almost unanimously rejected this way of raising revenue. Chamberlain's proposals seemed to offer an ingenious way round the seeming necessity to raise direct taxes to pay for welfare: make the foreigner pay as the phrase was coined and repeated. The revenue from imported goods could be used to pay for a Welfare State, without the necessity to increase direct taxation, as well as having the strongly positive effect of decreasing unemployment at home. (Critics of Chamberlain's proposals were not slow to point out the seemingly obvious flaw in his plans: if his tariffs kept out foreign goods, they would raise no revenue; but if they raised revenue, they would not have successfully kept out foreign goods.) Chamberlain's proposals had a particular appeal to particular parts of the economy, especially entrepreneurs in heavy industry and landowners, both of which had apparently suffered disproportionately in recent decades from Free Trade. Industrialists and manufacturers had lost ground to German and

American imports. Landowners and producers of foodstuffs and other agricultural goods had also felt severe competition from important foodstuffs after the introduction of refrigerated cargo ships in about 1880. Other business groups were less enthusiastic about his proposals, especially bankers, many shipowners, and those engaged in importing, who would presumably suffer from restrictions on free international trade.

Chamberlain's proposals also had a distinctive nationalistic and super-patriotic edge; indeed, they appeared xenophobic in rejecting the supposed benefits of Free Trade as engendering World Peace, mutually beneficial international commerce, and the steady progress and unity of mankind, which were among the ideological lynchpins of the deeply-held belief in Free Trade. Virtually all of Chamberlain's keenest supporters – certainly many of them – were on the right, even the far right, of the Unionist party on a variety of issues, then and in years to come. One keen supporter, Leo Maxse, the editor of the *National Review*, was an inveterate anti-German who has been accused (probably wrongly) of anti-semitism. Sir Henry Page Croft was often known as the 'most right wing' Conservative M.P. (no mean feat) in his long service in Parliament, and in 1917–22 founded and headed an ultra right wing group, the National Party. Lord Beaverbrook became virtually synonymous with right-wing politics, and, for instance, forty years later, was attacked as such by Clement Attlee in his radio broadcasts during the 1945 General Election. 'Little Englanders', believers in human progress, pacifists, and most social democrats eschewed Chamberlain's proposals from the moment they were enunciated, as did virtually all mainstream Liberals. Opponents of Tariff Reform also pointed out that his proposals entailed a 'tax on bread', which would fall heavily on the working classes, a contention which proved the proposal's electoral Achilles Heel for nearly thirty years. On the other hand, the majority of Tories supported Tariff Reform, including such future leaders of the party as Andrew Bonar Law and Stanley Baldwin. A minority of the Unionist party (as the coalition between the Conservatives and Liberal Unionists was officially known) did oppose it. Known as the 'Unionist Free Traders', they numbered about sixty-five M.P.s in late 1903 out of about 400 Unionist M.P.s. (Richard A. Rempel, *Unionists Divided: Arthur Balfour, Joseph Chamberlain and the Unionist Free Traders* (Newton Abbot, 1972), pp.225–6.) Many were Liberal Unionists rather than Conservatives. Most would come under increasing pressure from their local constituency associations, where party activists generally supported Chamberlain's proposals.

Tariff Reform thus had disproportionate support from certain specific components of the electorate. Margot Asquith – Herbert Asquith's wife, and thus an opponent of Tariff Reform – stated in 1922 that Chamberlain's proposals 'caught on like wildfire with the semi-clever, moderately educated, the Imperialists, Dukes, Journalists, and Fighting Men.' (Margot Asquith, *Autobiography, Volume II* (London, 1922), p.53, cited in Roy Jenkins, *Asquith* (London, 1967), p.151.n.l.) This takes us to the heart of the discussion in this chapter – and, indeed, throughout this book – since, omitting the first two groups included in Margot Asquith's critique – the one man in Britain who was closest to being an Imperialist, Duke, Journalist, and Fighting Man simultaneously was Winston Churchill, whose reaction to Tariff Reform was so negative that he left the Conservative party and joined the Liberals, the precise opposite of what one might have expected in advance, and, apparently, the precise opposite to the response of the great majority of those from his background. (Churchill was obviously not 'semi-clever', but he was arguably 'semi-educated', since he did not attend a university, entering Sandhurst after Harrow.) In other words, Churchill *should* have been an enthusiastic and outspoken adherent of Chamberlain's Tariff Reform cause. Instead, he moved in precisely the opposite direction. Remarkably, this apparently unaccountable sequence of events, seemingly so anomalous, has never been analysed as peculiar and strange, but has always been accepted by historians in a matter-of-fact manner, as if it were a natural part of Churchill's evolution as a politician. Nearly thirty years later, however, when Churchill was (again) a leading Conservative politician – indeed, one of the leaders of the 'die-hard' Tories – he accepted Tariff Reform and ceased to be a Free Trader.

Why did Churchill react so negatively to Chamberlain's proposals? A number of reasons might be offered. First, There is the motive of pure self-interest. Winston Churchill entered Parliament in September 1900 as Conservative M.P. for Oldham. His father had been the legendary Tory politician and, briefly, Chancellor of the Exchequer, his grandfather was a duke. Churchill was a war hero, a published author, and had already established a reputation as an outstanding speaker and orator. He was nearly twenty-six when Arthur Balfour resigned in December 1905 and a Liberal government formed. He was, by our standards, young to hold even junior office in Arthur Balfour's government, but, by the standards of the time, when young aristocrats and the scions of wealthy and landed families still entered Parliament at a young age, he was certainly not too young to be offered a junior office of some kind, given his lineage and talents. A number of aristocrats of about the same age as Churchill, including his relative the ninth Duke of Marlborough and the Earl of Donoughmore, had been given junior ministerial positions by Balfour, while Andrew Bonar Law, later Prime Minister, had been made Parliamentary Secretary to the Board of Trade in 1902 although, like Churchill, he had entered Parliament only two years earlier. Bonar Law, a dour New Brunswick-born Nonconformist iron merchant in Glasgow with a photographic memory for economic statistics, who had been educated in Glasgow High School but had not attended university, and who had no links whatever by background, education, marriage, or lifestyle with the traditional aristocracy, was a singularly anomalous – although inspired – choice by Balfour for a junior ministry so early in his parliamentary career, yet he was appointed. Despite his ancestry and brilliance, Churchill was not. Had Balfour offered Churchill even the most junior of ministerial posts, it is obviously difficult to imagine him changing parties. Churchill held no high opinion of Balfour, having written in a private letter as early as 1897 that 'I despise and detest' Balfour and also George Curzon (later Marquess Curzon), describing Balfour as 'a languid, lazy, lack-a-daisical cynic ... The unmonumental figurehead of the Conservative party' (cited in Roy Jenkins, *Churchill* (London, 2001), p.26), but politics makes strange bedfellows, and Churchill's attitude would presumably have changed had Balfour showed him proper regard. Why Balfour did not is a mystery, although the Unionist party (as the ruling alliance between the Conservatives and Liberal Unionists was known) had elected 402 M.P.s in 1900, in addition to its vast majority of supporters in the House of Lords, and doubtless had many potentially very able young men and newcomers from whom to choose for any vacancy. Nor could he know, in 1900–05, of Churchill's towering historical reputation. Balfour might already have seen Churchill as erratic and disloyal – he was already toying with the joining the Liberals – and as the heir to his father's notorious political instability. Nevertheless, had Balfour offered Churchill even the most minor of posts,

political history might have been very different. To
be sure, however, Churchill could not have known
that the Liberals would gain an overwhelming
parliamentary majority in 1906, and remain in
power, by itself or in coalition until 1922, or that
he would have held office for almost all of that
period, including the senior Cabinet posts of
First Lord of the Admiralty, Home Secretary, War
Minister, and Colonial Secretary. But he did believe
that the Tories were very likely to lose the next
General Election, writing to his American friend,
Bourke Cockran in December 1903 that 'I believe
that Chamberlain will be defeated at the General
Election by an overwhelming majority.' (Cited in
Randolph S. Churchill, *Winston S. Churchill: Volume
II – The Young Statesman* (London, 1967), p.72.)
Balfour's government was deeply and bitterly split
by the Tariff Reform debate as well as by its inept
handling of a number of other issues, alienating
Nonconformists by its 1902 Education Act and trade
unions by accepting the anti-union *Taff Vale* judicial
decision of 1901, which allowed trade unions to
be sued by employers for losses during a strike.

Britain's economy was not good, and the National Debt had increased because of the Boer War. It probably did not require a soothsayer to predict that the Liberals had a better-than-even chance of winning the next General Election. Between 1900 and 1905 the Unionists had lost twenty-six by-elections, but won only two, while the Liberals had won twenty and lost only four. Churchill can, then, reasonably be accused of a measure of self-interest and opportunism in his reaction to Tariff Reform and his switching parties, although plainly this was only a minor part of a much broader picture. It also seems at least arguable that a timely offer of a ministerial position by Balfour might have kept him in the Tory fold.

Another very personal element which must be taken into account in considering Churchill's opposition to Tariff Reform was his relationship with the memory of his late father, Lord Randolph Churchill (1849–95), and the shadow he continued to cast over his son well after his death. Churchill's relationship with his father is universally viewed by historians as unusually negative, even by the normal standards of fathers and sons with strong personalities. According to Lord Randolph's biographer, R.F. Foster, 'the doomed and embittered father alternately ignored and disliked his eldest son'. (*Lord Randolph Churchill: A Political Life* Oxford, 1981), p.383.) In contrast, Winston Churchill had an unusually close relationship with his mother, Jennie *nee* Jerome, the Brooklyn-born daughter of New York stockbroker and property developer. Lord Randolph Churchill died at the age of only forty-five, probably insane, possibly as a result of advanced syphilis, or (as most medical historians now believe), brain tumour. His lengthy period of mental instability made a profound impression on all political observers. Randolph Churchill *could* have been a major political figure, had he lived to a normal age, for another twenty-five years, and might well have become Tory leader in 1911 rather than Bonar Law. Randolph Churchill repeatedly flirted with 'Fair Trade', an earlier form of Tariff Reform which was widely discussed in the 1880s, long before Joseph Chamberlain's conversion to

Imperial Preference. That Winston Churchill's opposition to Chamberlain was motivated in part as a revolt against his father is quite possible. Foster (*Ibid.*, p.91) notes that in 1881 Lord Randolph 'came out firmly for Fair Trade' but his speech on this subject in Oldham was 'unmentioned in his son's biography', although he must have known about it. On the other hand, Randolph Churchill thought that he had been done in politically by Lord Salisbury and his nephew Arthur Balfour during the events which led to his resignation as Chancellor of the Exchequer late in 1886, a grudge which may well have affected his son's attitude towards Balfour. Randolph Churchill was also notoriously disloyal to his party's leadership, forming the so-called 'Fourth Party' as a ginger group to oppose Sir Stafford Northcote and the mainstream leaders of the Conservative party after their defeat at the 1880 General Election. Winston Churchill may well have believed his own disloyalty to the Tories echoed his father's actions, although, in actually joining the Liberals, they went far beyond them. Doubtless it is very difficult to arrive at any firm conclusions about the effects of the perpetual shadow of Lord Randolph Churchill which hung over Winston Churchill's career for so long, and psychological analysis but historians is always hazardous. Indeed, it was only after Winston Churchill had himself served as Chancellor of the Exchequer (in 1924–29) that he became one of the major leaders of the political right in Britain and fully accepted tariffs. Given Winston Churchill's supreme historical position, it is also difficult to remember that for the first several decades of his political career his father seemed the greater and more successful and important politician. Nevertheless, it seems clear that his relationship with his father was a factor in his opposition to Tariff Reform.

There were, however, many positive and ideologically distinctive elements in Winston Churchill's opposition to Chamberlain's programme, seemingly so unexpected. Churchill explained his opposition to Tariff Reform in a number of letters from 1903 which have been published in the Companion volumes to the official life of Winston

Churchill by Randolph S. Churchill and Martin Gilbert. It is useful to report salient parts, for they set out Churchill's thinking at the very beginnings of Chamberlain's Tariff Reform campaign, and when he was in the process of becoming a Liberal. In chronological order, these are:

Churchill to J. Moore Bayley, 20 May 1903

... The only way in which we can help the Colonies is by paying duties on raw materials and foodstuffs – the very commodities taxation of which cannot be of the slightest use or value to the manufacturer.

Is it conceivable that the manufacturer will be content to bear this burden all by himself and let both English agriculturalists and Colonial producers gain the benefit? No, he will infallibly demand a *quid pro quo*; and as surely as we embark upon the slippery path of protection, we shall finish up amid a tangle of high protective tariffs of all kinds. If that be so, exit for ever the banking, broking, warehousing predominance of Great Britain.

I do not want a selfcontained Empire. It is very much better that the great nations of the world should be interdependent one upon the other than that they should be independent of each other. That makes powerfully for peace and it is chiefly through the cause of the great traffic of one great nation with another during the last twenty five years that the peace of Europe has been preserved through so many crises.

And even if it comes to an European War, do you not think it very much better that the United States should be vitally interested in keeping the English market open, than that they should be utterly careless of what happens to their present principal customer?

Churchill to Arthur Balfour, 25 May 1903
I am utterly opposed to anything which will alter the Free Trade character of this country; & I consider such an issue superior in importance to any other now before us. … I am persuaded that once this policy is begun it must lead to

the establishment of a complete Protective system, involving commercial disaster, & the Americanisation of English politics. I do not now attempt to argue all this. But I submit these two points to you: 1. From a national point of view there is no case for a fiscal revolution … 2. From a party point of view the government is probably less unpopular than any which has ruled 8 years in England.

Churchill to J.H. Lawton, 1 July 1903
Protection is, in the first instance, undoubtedly beneficial to the protected trade whatever it may be. It is secured from foreign competition and can enjoy a practical monopoly of the Home Market. This advantage is however obtained at the expense of the general consumer, who, being deprived of his right to buy in the cheapest market, has to pay rather more for home made goods, and, in the second place, the quality of the goods is apt to deteriorate under the unhealthy conditions of monopoly. It may be urged that there is enough competition

within the country to prevent these evils, or, at any rate, to prevent anything like a monopoly being established, but I would point out to you that the natural consequence of protection is an attempt on the part of the manufacturers to form trusts, and as they are often able to agree among themselves, the great development of the Trust system, which we have seen with such striking results in the United States, may easily follow.

Now it should be remembered that what happens in the case of one protected trade may happen in the case of all protected trades. Therefore the consumer will pay more for the articles which he uses and will perhaps not get such good articles in the end. His loss will be more or less severe in proportion to the amount of protection given and to the number of industries protected. But the consumer's loss does not stop with the consumer. It operates in two ways upon trade generally. In the first place, by making the cost of living higher, it increases the cost of production and consequently hampers our competition in the neutral, foreign and Imperial markets, and when we think that a great portion of our export trade is absorbed by native populations in India, China and Africa, it must be clear to you that cheapness of production is a matter of almost vital importance. And this is particularly true of the Cotton Trade which constitutes one fourth of all our exports, and which has to depend and will increasingly have to depend upon the demand of the less civilised and native population of the world.

Secondly the increased cost of living to the consumer reduces the general demand for commodities. He has spent more money on this or that manufactured article because it is a protected article, he has therefore less money left to spend on other things. So much for the general theory which underlies the position adopted by Free Traders in regard to Free Trade. We do not deny that industries may be made to flourish by artificial means in the power of the State to administer, but we contend that the Government must look to the wellbeing of the country as a whole not to that of any particular class or section and we believe that if a Government honestly pursues the greatest good of the greatest number, they will have established a system of society which will be more favourable than any other to the development of special interests and which will secure the supremacy of the best.

It is often urged that by threatening to tax foreign manufactured articles we might persuade foreign nations to admit ours free, and this is what the reciprocitrians and retaliationists desire, or affect to desire. But these methods of retaliation have been tried by all the protectionist countries for generations, and the result is that so far from arriving at free trade, they have only raised their tariffs higher and higher. And today we, the one free country in the world, are, in relation to all the other nations of the world, no worse off but are better off for trading purposes than any of the protected nations, for we enjoy with nearly every country the most favoured nation treaty; and although I should be far from saying that this treaty was always observed faithfully by other countries, yet in the balance its advantages are very great.

Churchill to Colonel J. Mitford, 9 July 1903

Of course it stands to reason that we are all in favour of the consolidation of the British Empire, of compelling foreign nations to adopt Free Trade and of increasing British commercial prosperity; and if Mr Chamberlain's fiscal proposals can be shown to produce these desirable ends, they would claim wide if not universal support. But I should like to point out to you that so far as this controversy has advanced, Mr Chamberlain, although he has enlarged upon many benefits which we should all desire, has made no definite proposal by which these benefits can be secured, and I myself as a Conservative Free Trader gravely doubt whether any fiscal change will bring them within our reach. I fear that a policy of

Preferential Tariffs will lead to much friction between the Colonies and the mother country, and if it is based upon the taxation of food, will estrange the masses of our countrymen from the Imperial idea.

Retaliation has been tried by all the protectionist nations for many years, and so far from arriving at free trade, they have only raised their tariff walls higher and higher; and even now Free Trade England has better terms in respect of all other countries of the world taken together than any one of the highly protected states.

Thirdly, I would look to improvements in scientific and technical education, to light taxation, to pacific policy and to a stable and orderly state of Society, as the best means of stimulating the commercial prosperity of our country. But the burden of proof is admitted to rest with Mr Chamberlain and his supporters. They invite the richest nation in the world to change its fiscal system. They have first of all to prove that the old system has failed.; they have in the second place, to state plainly and definitely the new system they propose to establish, and in the third place, they have to show that their new system will in fact achieve the ends they have in view and work a real and substantial improvement in our condition. Until they have done these things, Free Traders are not called upon to put forward any alternative scheme for we are in the position of adhering to the principles which have been long accepted in this country.

Churchill to J.T. Travis-Clegg
But, like all the advocates of quack remedies, he protests too much. Nobody is to suffer, everybody is to gain. Employment will be regular, wages will rise. The miller is to be protected. The labourer will return to the land. In Ireland two pigs are to grow where one grew before. Sugar refining will revive at Greenock. There will be a boom in Rochester cement. The cost of food will remain unaltered, but those who sell it are to get a

better price. Manufacturers will make larger profits, but the consumer will pay no more. By a proposal so small as not to dislocate our trade our industries are to be sustained and our Empire consolidated and without any extra charge to the taxpayer the Exchequer will be embarrassed every year with a mighty surplus. How is to be done? It is as easy as thimble-rigging. All is to be paid by the dirty foreigner, all except a tax on bacon. Apparently the foreigner will not pay a tax on bacon. It is the food of the poor, and perhaps for that very reason the foreigner – who will pay all the others – with callous villainy refuses to pay it. And here, again, is an argument for retaliation. It is a wonderful plan. Will the people be taken in? I think not. Labouring men must view with unalterable suspicion a scheme for reducing the cost of living by taxing every mouthful they eat. The Colonies will reject proposals to cramp their economic development, like the Chinese women tie up their children's feet. The commercial classes will shrink from the disturbance of an utterly unnecessary revolution. And trade unionists will not be such fools as to hand themselves over to capitalist combinations at the very moment when, owing to the state of the law, they have lost much of the power and freedom which Lord Beaconsfield intended them to have. I have not concealed from you my opposition. I hold that, though free trade, like every other policy, has its defects in this imperfect world, still on the whole the abundance of commodities, the simplicity of our Customs arrangements, the freedom of our ports, the adaptiveness of our industries, the purity of our public life give to our workers much more than foreign nations are able to gain by tariff juggles, usually stupid, often corrupt.

Churchill was making four or five major points. First, in the long term Protection always harmed the country imposing tariffs, by raising prices and diminishing choice; secondly, tariffs might benefit British manufacturing but harm British finance and commerce – the 'banking, broking, and warehousing predominance of Great Britain'; thirdly, Imperial Preference would crucially harm Britain's relations with the United States, especially if a war came in which American support was sought; fourthly, tariffs would bring with them the 'Americanisation of English politics', with massive lobbying by interest groups for tariff support such as routinely occurred in the United States; fifthly, that British tariffs would harm what is now called the 'Third World'; and, lastly, that Britain should not lightly abandon a fiscal system which brought it economic greatness.

Although Churchill's fears that American-style lobbying would become ingrained in Britain are well-known and often cited by biographers, his other points are less well-known and deserve some comment. Churchill was half-American and was already a familiar figure in the United States, having visited America in 1895 and made an extensive five month lecture tour in North America in 1990–01 which took him to New York, Boston, Chicago,

St. Louis, Washington, and Baltimore. (Martin Gilbert, *Churchill and America* (London, 2005), pp.18–44.) His closest friend there, who became a kind of father figure to him, was a little-known Irish-born Democratic Congressman, Bourke Cockran, an advocate of Irish Home Rule. (*Ibid.*, pp.21–30.) Many decades later, Churchill also told American Presidential candidate Adlai Stevenson that Cockran had been the most influential single person in teaching Churchill how to speak successfully in public. (*Ibid.*, p.17.) What most distinguished the Democratic from the Republican parties at the time, it is now easy to forget, was their attitudes towards tariffs: Democrats favoured low or no tariffs; Republicans were in favour of – and in power enacted – high tariff walls. Churchill was impressed by America, although many aspects of American society, from its paper money (unknown as yet in Britain) and the 'vulgarity' of its press, were jarring. (*Ibid.*, pp.15–16.) Yet it is clear that Churchill was also already thinking in terms of policies which would win friends and supporters in the United States rather than alienate it. The

possibility of tariffs alienating the United States
had been made by Free Traders even before
Chamberlain's 1903 speech, although privately, as
in a memorandum in November 1902 from Edward
Hamilton, the Assistant Secretary to the Treasury (a
civil service position) to C.T. Ritchie, the pro-Free
Trade Chancellor of the Exchequer (Rempel, *op.cit.*,
p.17), although Churchill appears to have given
it special centrality, in light of his life-long and
arguably unique advocacy of a Special Relationship
between Britain and the United States, and, beyond
them, among the 'English-speaking peoples'.

The other point which requires some comment
is Churchill's concern that British finance and
commerce would suffer under a tariff regime.
Churchill was thus dividing the main sectors
of Britain's economy between manufacturing
and industry on the one hand, and finance and
commerce on the other. Churchill's insight that
finance and commerce was highly important to
the British economy had been endorsed by many
recent economic historians; arguably it was more

important than manufacturing and industry. The relative absence of bankers and figures in commerce, such as shipowners, from the inner circle of keen Tariff Reformers was widely remarked upon at the time. (See, for instance, Andrew Marrison, *British Business and Protection, 1903–1932* (Oxford, 1996), esp. pp.201–204.) Although the City of London as a political constituency remained strongly pro-Tory and never supported the Liberals after the 1870s, many City figures unquestionably believed that Free Trade and its continuation were central to the maintenance of the City's role as the most important international financial and commercial centre in the world. It might also be noted that Churchill's virtually unknown brother Jack (d.1947) was a stockbroker in the City of London, and might have given him advice. Churchill, of course, personally had no business or commercial experience in the strict sense, although his views on the sources of wealth generation in the British economy seem very perceptive. Chamberlain himself, as is well-known, was a screw manufacturer in Birmingham and many of his supporters (not all, of course) were industrialists in heavy industry who had been especially hard hit by foreign imports. Landowners and farmers also flocked to his banner for the same reason.

Churchill also addressed the questions of Tariff Reform and Free Trade in numerous formal speeches in Parliament and to outside audiences from 1903 to 1905. He made eight speeches on these questions in 1903, fourteen in 1904, and seven in 1905. (Robert Rhodes James, ed., *Winston S. Churchill – His Complete Speeches, 1897–1963, Volume I: 1897–1908* (New York, 1974), pp.157–519, *passim.*) His pro-Free Trade and anti-Protectionist remarks in these were more predictable and when on the platform often oriented towards the gallery. He told an audience at Birmingham Town Hall on 11 November 1903 – a brave appearance in Chamberlain's very inner sanctum – that 'I am not in the least disconcerted when people say that they have had enough of the 'clap-trap' about cheap food for the people ... It might be clap-trap to the millionaire proprietors of a dozen newspapers (laughter), but to the workingman's wife who has to make a week's wages balance the week's bills a half-penny up here or a penny up there is not clap-trap at all, but one of the most grim and grinding necessities of life. (Cheers.)' (*Ibid.*, p.221.) Churchill also claimed that foreign goods were often 'dumped in Britain (sold below cost) because high prices at home, brought about by their own tariffs, meant they could not be sold in their own country. 'Under the beneficent system of Protection,' he told an audience at Park Hall, Cardiff, on 1 December 1903, 'the German manufacturer has learned to do business at a loss. It is an expensive way of getting rich.' (*Ibid.*, p.220.)

Adding all of this up, however, it is still very arguable whether these reasons together really account for Churchill's switch of parties. This is particularly true because the subject on which he chose to make the defining issue seems so anomalous – the arch-imperialist, the soldier, the believer in British greatness, leaving the Conservative party over a programme which was designed to facilitate these ends, not over some destructive proposal. Churchill's actions in 1903–05 are among the most anomalous of his career.

Churchill continued to be a keen Free Trader until about 1930. Between 1924 and 1929 he was Chancellor of the Exchequer, a most unexpected appointment by Stanley Baldwin after the Tories decisively won the October 1924 General Election, replacing Ramsay Macdonald's short-lived minority Labour government. By 1924, Churchill had again become a Tory. He remained a Coalition Liberal until he was defeated at the 1922 General Election (when, at Dundee, a two member seat, he finished with the fourth highest total vote). After one unsuccessful attempt to contest Leicester West as a Liberal in the December 1923 general election, Churchill then became, first a 'Constitutionalist', contesting a famous by-election at the Abbey Westminster constituency in early1924 under that label, and then a full-dress and official Conservative, being elected as an M.P. again at the Epping, Essex (in suburban London) at the 1924 General Election. Baldwin's offer of the Number Two position in the Cabinet to a former leading Liberal who had, moreover, deserted the Conservatives and who had, during the First World War, proven highly unpopular with most Tory politicians, was to many assuredly a curious if not inexplicable act. Churchill, moreover, had no business or commercial experience or knowledge of finance. Baldwin was, it seems, motivated by two main factors. He had contested the 1923 General Election on a policy of Protectionism and, as in 1906, had seen the Tories defeated after charges of 'dear bread' and 'a tax on food' had cost them many working-class seats. (At the 1922 General Election, the Conservatives had elected 345 M.P.s; the National Liberals (pro-Lloyd George) 62; the Liberals (pro-Asquith) 54; and Labour 142. At the 1923 General Election, the next to be held, the Conservatives elected 258 M.P.s; the Liberals 159; and Labour 191. It was then that Macdonald was asked to form the first Labour government. After the failure of the minority Labour government, the Tories contested the October 1924 general election promising not to enact tariffs. It then elected 419 M.P.s, compared with151 Labourites and only 40 Liberals. Baldwin almost certainly appointed Churchill, a well-known Free Trader who had left the Tories twenty years before over this issue, to signal that the party was serious when it said it did not intend to enact Tariff Reform. Churchill was also appointed as a signal by Baldwin that former Liberals would be received with open arms by the Conservatives as their former party collapsed, and that the Tories now represented the only realistic alternative to Socialism. He was also doubtless motivated by the desire to thwart any Liberal alliance between Churchill and Lloyd George. As well, whatever one might think at this point of Churchill as a political figure, he was unquestionably brilliant and eloquent, one of the best speakers in public life, and a great catch for the party.

Churchill's time as Chancellor is almost always regarded by historians as a failure, marked by permanently high levels of unemployment despite the prosperity of the 1920s and, of course, by the General Strike of May 1926. In particular, Churchill's decision in April 1925 to return to the Gold Standard at the fixed gold party rate of £1 = \$4.86 is looked upon as a colossal mistake, making British exports more expensive and increasing unemployment. It might also be viewed as the victory of the City of London over the manufacturing industry; as we have seen, Churchill was long favourable to the centrality of the City and of finance and commerce rather than to manufacturing.

It is, however, well-known that as Chancellor Churchill fought a consistent rear-guard action in the Cabinet against the general principle of enacting tariffs, which was still demanded by many Tories in a government with a huge majority. As Chancellor, however, he did make two 'minor infringements' of this doctrine, to enact imperial preference on some goods imported from the Empire and on the 'safeguarding' of industries against 'unfair' foreign competition. (Paul Addison, *Churchill on the Home Front, 1900–1955* (London, 1993), p.243.) According to Paul Addison, however (*Ibid.*, p.250), 'Churchill's principal achievement at the Treasury was to hold the line in defence of Free Trade.' He 'threatened to resign in the event of a protectionist duty on steel." (*Ibid.*, p.251.)

This stage in Churchill's career may be seen as transitional, for, around 1930, he became a committed Protectionist, apparently dropping all opposition to Tariff Reform. 'In October 1930" Addison states bluntly, 'he abandoned the cause of Free Trade, the one principle to which he had clung tenaciously throughout all the twists and turns of his career.' (*Ibid.*, p.288.) In 1932, when Neville Chamberlain, Joe's son and now Chancellor of the Exchequer, actually introduced an Import Duties Bill to enact Protection, Churchill frankly admitted that his previous fears about corruption following the introduction of tariffs had been groundless. 'There has been no scramble of great interests, no log-rolling, bribery, or corruption, none!' he told the House of Commons in May 1932. (Cited in *Ibid.*, p.305.) For the rest of his long career, Churchill accepted the necessity for the Sterling Bloc and other restrictions on Victorian Free Trade.

Churchill's conversion at this time – which certainly requires a detailed, scholarly study – must be seen in the context of his move to the far right of politics on a wide variety of fronts, especially over moves towards some measure of Indian self-determination, and his detestation of Communism. During the next few years after the Tories left office in 1929, Churchill again reinvented himself as the leading right-wing 'Die-hard' politician in Britain, an ally of the fierce anti-Bolshevist, anti-colonial independence spokesmen on the Tory back benches, in the Tory press, and in Tory constituency associations. As in 1900–05, ambition and spite may have played a role in his shift: Churchill was probably the most high-profile figure (along with Lloyd George) excluded from the 1931 National government headed by the former Labour Prime Minister Ramsay Macdonald, but dominated by the overwhelming Tory majority in Parliament after the 1931 General Election. Until1940 Churchill sat on the back benches, where, of course, from the mid-1930s, he became leader of the anti-Appeasement forces and became set on the path to immortality as the greatest of British political leaders. The Churchill who became Prime Minister in May 1940 was, I many respects, a Tory 'Die-hard', who famously said, in November 1932, that 'I have not become the King's first Minister in order to preside over the liquidation of the British Empire', and, in the 1945 General Election campaign, claimed that a Labour government "would have to fall back on some form of Gestapo, or 'political force' to establish Socialism." Few would have realised that this was the same man who left the Conservative party forty years earlier because of his deep commitment to Free Trade and Liberal values. There were, of course, many continuities in Churchill's beliefs, especially his deep commitment to the Anglo-American alliance and his hostility to Labour precisely because it seemed to be authoritarian and anti-liberal. Perhaps because of this, however, the anomalousness of Churchill's position over Chamberlain's tariff proposals forty years earlier has never received the attention it deserves.

Chapter Two

CHURCHILL
AND
BOLSHEVISM

FROM SOON AFTER THE BOLSHEVIK
Revolution in the late 1917, and emphatically
from 1919, Winston Churchill became probably
the fiercest critic of Bolshevism and of the Soviet
government in the British mainstream, certainly
apart from the recognised spokesmen and organs of
the extreme right. This may now seem unsurprising
to us, as we are likely to view Churchill as a

Conservative and Tory icon, to recall his opposition to Stalinist expansionism at Yalta, and his celebrated 'Iron Curtain' at Fulton, Missouri in March 1946 which helped to set off the Cold War. However from the viewpoint of the years immediately after the Bolshevik Revolution, such a supposition is, on the contrary, highly surprising. In 1917 Churchill was not a Tory, but a committed Liberal with an acknowledged track record of sincere support for the Liberal Party and the 'New Liberalism' of Asquith and Lloyd George. Yet, to employ the current vernacular, Churchill 'went ballistic' over the Bolshevik Revolution. His response to it was so extreme as to mark him out from most other British politicians not already on the far right, and was an important factor in his evolution from a centre-left Liberal to a right-wing Tory. As with Churchill's response to Tariff Reform, however, his extreme reaction to Bolshevism has probably not received the attention it deserves.

In the years between his joining the Liberal Party in 1903–05 and the Bolshevik Revolution, Churchill had carved out an important record as a leading Liberal politician, and was unquestionably seen by the general public and by informed commentators as a man of the centre-left. As President of the Board of Trade between April 1908 and February 1910, Churchill had introduced many social reforms, including labour exchanges, support for unemployment insurance, and wages boards to regulate pay in sweatshops. (Paul Addison, *Churchill on the Home Front, 1900–1955* (London, 1993), pp.74–81.) He supported Lloyd George's 'People's Budget' of 1909, higher direct taxes on the rich, and an end to the House of Lords' veto powers. As Home Secretary from February 1910 until October 1911, he reprieved nearly half of murderers sentenced to death, a higher percentage than his contemporaries, and pursued an active agenda of prison reform. (*Ibid.*, pp.110–119.) Almost literally until the day the First World War broke out, Churchill was a vocal proponent of Irish Home Rule. At a major speech on this question at Bradford in March 1914, he stated that 'there is no lawful measure from which the Government should shrink, and there is no lawful measure from which it will shrink' in suppressing violence by Ulster Unionists. (Robert Rhodes James, ed., *Winston S. Churchill – His Complete Speeches, 1897–1963, Volume III, 1914–1922* (New York, 1974), p.2230.) In the same speech he accused Sir Edward Carson and the Ulster Unionists of being engaged in a 'treasonable conspiracy'. (*Ibid.*, p.2228.) As we have seen, Churchill was an active supporter of Free Trade and an outspoken opponent of Tariff Reform. During the First World War, he famously advocated victory by a 'sideshow' such as the ill-fated Gallipoli campaign, in large measure to spare the lives of the tens of thousands pointlessly mowed down on the Western Front, making himself highly unpopular with the Conservative Party as a result. There are aspects of Churchill's record which suggest a more varied ideological picture, such as his opposition to general female suffrage (as opposed to limited suffrage for women graduates and the highly educated), and his suppression of strikes in Wales and Scotland, but it seems unarguable that from 1905 through 1917, Churchill was, to reiterate, a committed man of the centre-left and opposed right-wing Tory policies and the Tory party on a range of issues. His response to the early years of the Bolshevik Revolution might be expected to be one of welcoming some of its reforms, while rejecting its extremism, and trying to accommodate the Soviet government into the new, postwar European order as quickly as possible.

Instead, from the time of the Bolshevik Revolution Churchill quickly emerged as probably the most extreme anti-Bolshevik in the British mainstream. His only equals in this respect were arguably those on the very extreme right of British political life, often over the edge of the mainstream – right-wing Tories such as Sir Henry Page Croft and the Duke of Northumberland, right-wing newspapers such as the *Morning Post*, crackpot 'conspiracy theorists' such as Nesta Webster, and H.H. Beamish, many of whom at this time were explicitly anti-semitic, or linked Jews with Germany as the progenitors of Bolshevism, whose aim appeared to be to extinguish not merely capitalism but democracy and all aspects of traditional Russian society and which pulled Russia, an ally of Britain and France under both Tsarist and Kerensky governments, out of the War, surrendering vast swathes of western Russia to Germany and freeing up hundreds of thousands of German troops for use on the Western front in 1917–18. But Churchill's attitude towards Bolshevism, by a politician who was, to reiterate, emphatically on the centre-left rather than the far right, was so extreme as to be highly anomalous.

Probably Churchill's most considered and extreme attack on Bolshevism in the years immediately after the Bolshevik Revolution came in a speech made to the Aldwych Club Luncheon at the Connaught Rooms, London, on 11 April 1919. At the time, Churchill was in the Cabinet as Minister for War and Air, a post he held from 10 January 1919 until 13 February 1921, at which time he was masterminding British support for the 'White' anti-Bolshevik armies, a fact which should be kept in mind in considering his rhetoric. Nevertheless, it is so extreme that it deserves to be quoted at length:

(From Robert Rhodes James, ed., *Winston S. Churchill – His Complete Speeches 1897–1963, Volume II, 1914–1922* (New York, 1974), pp.2771–2772)

I only wish that the march of events on the Continent had been as favourable as in our own island. On the contrary, the process of degeneration has been steady and even rapid over large parts of Europe. The British Government has issued a White-book giving a vivid picture, based on authentic evidence, of Bolshevist atrocities. Tyranny presents itself in many forms. The British nation is the foe of tyranny in every form. That is why we fought Kaiserism and that is why we would fight it again. That is why we are opposing Bolshevism. Of all tyrannies in history the Bolshevist tyranny is the worst, the most destructive, and the most degrading. It is sheer humbug to pretend that it is not" far worse than German militarism. The miseries of the Russian people under the Bolshevists far surpass anything they suffered even under the Tsar. The atrocities by Lenin and Trotsky are incomparably more hideous, on a larger scale, and more numerous than any for which the Kaiser himself is responsible. There is this also to be remembered-whatever crimes the Germans have committed, and we have not spared them in framing our indictment, at any rate they stuck to their Allies. They misled them, they exploited them, but they did not desert, or betray them. It may have been honour among thieves, but that is better than dishonour among murderers.

Lenin and Trotsky had no sooner seized on power than they dragged the noble Russian nation out of the path of honour and let loose on us and our Allies a whole deluge of German reinforcements, which burst on us in March and April of last year. Every British and French soldier killed last year was really done to death by Lenin and Trotsky, not in fair war, but by the treacherous desertion of an ally without parallel in the history of the world. There are still Russian Armies in the field, under Admiral Koltchak and General Deniken, who have never wavered in their faith and loyalty to the Allied cause, and who are fighting valiantly and by no means unsuccessfully against that foul combination of criminality and animalism which constitutes the Bolshevist *regime.* We are helping these men, within the limits which are assigned to us, to the very best of our ability. We are helping them with arms and munitions, with instructions and technical experts, who volunteered for service. It would not be right for us to send our armies raised on a compulsory basis to Russia. If Russia is to be saved it must be by Russian manhood. But all our hearts are with these men who are true to the Allied cause in their splendid struggle to restore the honour of united Russia, and to rebuild on a modern and democratic basis the freedom, prosperity, and happiness of its trustful and good-hearted people.

There is a class of misguided or degenerate people in this country and some others, who profess to take so lofty a view that they cannot see any difference between what they call rival Russian factions. They would have you believe that it is "six of one and half-a-dozen of the other." Their idea of a League of Nations is something which would be impartial as between Bolshevism on the one hand, and civilization on the other. We are still forced to distinguish between right and wrong, loyalty and treachery, health and disease, progress and anarchy. There is one part of the world in which these distinctions which we are bound to draw can translate itself into action. In the North of Russia the Bolshevists are continually attacking the British troops we sent there during the course of the war against Germany in order to draw off the pressure from the West, and who are now cut off by the ice from the resources of their fellow countrymen. Here we are in actual warfare with the representatives of a Bolshevist Government and with its Army, and, whatever views may be held by any section in the country on Russian affairs, we must all agree that our men who were sent there by the Government have to be properly supported and relieved from their dangerous situation. (Cheers.) We have no intention whatever of deserting our lads and of leaving them on this icy shore to the mercy of a cruel foe. The Prime Minister has given me the fullest authority to take whatever measures the General Staff of the Army think necessary to see that our men are relieved, and brought safely through the perils with which they are confronted, and so far as is physically possible we shall take whatever measures are required. (Cheers.)

So grave was the danger to Western civilisation from Bolshevism Churchill went on, that

(From *Ibid., p.2773*)
A way of atonement is open to Germany. By combating Bolshevism, by being the bulwark against it, Germany may take the first step toward ultimate reunion with the civilized world. I am sure the advice you would

receive from those gifted soldiers who have conducted our Armies to victory would be to feel Germany, to make Germany do her share in clearing up the mess and ruin her Imperialistic Government has caused, and to stand by meanwhile, with a strong British and Allied Army on the Rhine, to guard against foul play or any failure to comply with our just and reasonable demands.

Very great perils still menace us in the world. Two mighty branches of the human race, the Slavs and the Teutons, are both plunged at the present time in the deepest misery. The Great Power which was our foe, and the great Power which was our friend, are both in the pit of ruin and despair. It is extremely undesirable that they should come together. Germany is struggling against breaking down into Bolshevism. But if that were to happen it would produce reaction which it is no exaggeration to say would reach as far as China.

The Russian Bolshevist revolution is changing in its character. It has completed the

Anarchist destruction of the social order in Russia itself. The political, economic, social, and moral life of the people of Russia has for the time being been utterly smashed. Famine and terror are the order of the day. Only the military structure is growing out of the ruin. That is still weak, but it is growing steadily stronger, and it is assuming an aggressive and predatory form, which French Jacobinism assumed after the fall of Robespierre, and before the rise of Napoleon. Bolshevist armies are marching on towards food and plunder, and in their path stand only the little weak States, exhausted and shattered by the war.

Churchill thus viewed Bolshevism as very much the successor to the French Jacobins during the Reign of Terror, only much worse, and, presciently, he foresaw an alliance between Germany and the Soviet Union such as emerged a few years later with the Rapallo Treaty and n the Nazi-Soviet Pact of 1939, also foreseeing the extreme dangers of this alliance to the democracies.

On 3 January 1920, in a speech at Victoria Hall, Sunderland, Churchill again turned to the theme of Bolshevism and its dangers, in similarly extreme terms:

(From Robert Thodes James, *Ibid.*, pp.2918–2920 (extracts))

There is another class which, in my judgment, it is no use our trying to conciliate. I mean those Bolshevists, fanatics who are the avowed enemies of the existing civilization of the world – (A voice: "It's a lie.") –, who if they had their way would destroy the democratic parliaments on which the liberties of free peoples depend, and would also shatter the economic and scientific apparatus by which alone the great millions of modern populations can be maintained alive. So far from conciliating these people and trying to make them believe that we are going in the same direction as they are, only not quite so fast and not quite so far, we ought to take every opportunity of going for them – (laughter and cheers) – of discrediting them of exposing them to the nation, of showing how enormous and unbridgeable is the gulf which separates them from us. We believe in Parliamentary Government exercised in accordance with the – will of the majority of the electors constitutionally and freely ascertained. They seek to overthrow Parliament by direct action or other violent means.

… Was there ever a more awful spectacle in the whole history of the world than is unfolded by the agony of Russia? This vast country, this mighty branch of the human family, not only produced enough food for itself, but, before the war, it was one of the great granaries of the world, from which food was exported to every country. It is now reduced to famine of the most terrible kind, not because there is no food-there is plenty of food-but because the theories of Lenin and Trotsky have fatally, and it may be finally, ruptured the means of intercourse between man and man, between workman and peasant, between town and country; because they have shattered the systems of scientific communication by rail and river on which the life of great cities depends; because they have raised class against class and race against race in fratricidal war; because they have given vast regions where a little while ago were smiling villages or prosperous townships back to the wolves and the bears; because they have driven man from the civilization of the 20th century into a condition of barbarism worse than the Stone Age, and have left him the most awful and pitiable spectacle in human experience, devoured by vermin, racked by pestilence, and deprived of hope.

And this is progress, this is liberty, this is Utopia! This is what my friend in the gallery would call an interesting experiment in social regeneration. (Laughter.) What a monstrous absurdity and perversion of the truth it is to represent the communistic theory as a form of progress when, at every step and at every stage, it is simply marching back into the dark ages. That gallant soldier and stalwart

Labour man, Colonel John Ward, who has seen these things with his own eyes – (A voice– "He has not.") – who, I say, has seen these things for many months with his own eyes, and has played an honourable part on every occasion, has summed all up in one biting, blasting phrase – "Back to the jungle." "Ah! but," say the Bolshevists and the sympathisers of the Bolshevists, and the panderers of the Bolshevists, and the would-be imitators in this country of the Bolshevists, "they have not 'had a fair chance…there has been so much disorder that Comrade Lenin and Comrade Trotsky have not had an opportunity of carrying their theories smoothly and peaceably into effect." They can never have such a chance, and for this grave and vital reason, that the theories that have held are fundamentally opposed to the needs and dictates of the human heart, and of human nature itself. (A voice – "What about self-determination?) They are fatally opposed to self-determination. (Cheers.) My friend has not been studying this with sufficient attention.

He probably thinks that the Bolshevists overthrew the Tsar. That is absolutely untrue. They overthrew the Russian Republic. What was the first step they took? It was to destroy the Russian Parliament, to put the greater number of its members to death. What did Litvinoff say when he met Mr. O'Grady at Copenhagen? He said, "We admit we have not got a majority of our country. We are not prepared to hold a constituent assembly, we are not prepared to allow any interference in the internal affairs of Russia."…

In other words, by April 1919, eighteen months after the Bolshevik Revolution, Churchill was already claiming that 'Of all the tyrannies in history the Bolshevist tyranny is the worst, the most destructive, and the most degrading … incomparably more hideous, on a larger scale, than any for which the Kaiser was responsible.' Churchill's gut hostility to Bolshevism began even earlier, and one can document a long list of extreme attacks on Bolshevism from no later than February

1918. On 23 February 1918, Churchill wrote to Lord Beaverbrook that 'I am increasingly convinced that there can be no more valuable propaganda [to British workers] in England at the present time than graphic accounts of the Bolshevist outrages and futility, of the treacheries they have committed, and what ruin they have brought upon their country and the harm they have done to us and to our fighting men.' (Martin Gilbert, *Winston S. Churchill: Volume IV – Companion Part I – Documents January1917- June 1919* (London, 1977), p.250). On 3 August 1918 he wrote in a draft letter to Sir George Ritchie (in a letter apparently never sent), 'Russia is in the deepest abyss. ... Nothing has ever been seen like the awful misery and convulsion of Russia.' (*Ibid.*, p.365). When Royal Navy Captain Francis Cromie was murdered by the Bolsheviks in August 1918, Churchill stated in a Cabinet memorandum which was not circulated, 'The only policy which is likely to be effective, either for the past or the future, is to mark down the personalities of the Bolshevik Government as the objects upon whom justice will be executed, however long it takes, and to make them feel that their punishment will become an important object of British policy.' (*Ibid.*, pp.382–383.) Churchill wrote to his constituents in Dundee – his unlikely parliamentary seat at the time – on 13 December 1918, as part of his reelection campaign in the 1918 General Election that 'This is no time for feeble compromises … (L)et us go forward against the foes of Scotland and Britain, whether they be the Huns abroad or the pacifists, Bolsheviks, and Sinn Feiners at home…' – an untypical piece of Churchillian populism. (*Ibid.*, pp.435–6.) Mary Spiers (the wife of Brigadier General Sir Edward Spiers) noted in her diary on 24 January 1919, 'Winston told LG [Lloyd George] one might as well legalize sodomy as recognize the Bolsheviks.' (*Ibid.*, p.479.) Many other similar comments can be found throughout Churchill's speeches, letters, and remarks at this time.

As noted, Churchill did more than rant against the Bolshevik regime. He was largely responsible, as Britain's War Minister, for launching British military intervention against the Bolsheviks. This intervention began in June–August 1918, before Churchill became War Minister in January 1919, but Churchill did everything possible to augment the intervention of British and foreign troops in Russia in support of the anti-Bolshevik 'Whites', which lasted until September 1919. By that time, the domestic anti-war mood, the opposition of Labour, and the failures and inadequacies of the 'White' forces and leaders, and the need for budget economies, made further intervention impossible. Many foreign countries, including France, the United States, Poland, and Japan, assisted the anti-Bolshevik forces, but the anti-war mood after the Armistice made successful intervention impossible. Although we now strongly associate the infamous mass murders committed during the Soviet period with Stalin, especially during the 1930s, it is important to realise that the Russian Civil War of 1917–21 was accompanied by extreme brutality on both sides, with the Soviet Secret Police already responsible for extraordinary numbers of murders and reprisals. According to Micheal (*sic*) Clodfelter, *Warfare and Armed Conflict: A Statistical Reference to Casualty and Other Figures, 1500–2000* (Jefferson, N.C., 2002, p.386), 'The security police of both sides – the notorious Soviet Cheka under Feliks (*sic*) Dzerzhinksi in particular – may have killed as many as 1 million Russians through execution or imprisonment. Another half million Russians died in the long Siberian retreat of 1919–20 … All told, as many as *9 million* Russians may have died as a result of the turmoil and upheaval of the Russian Civil War.' (My italics.) It might incidentally be noted that the extreme brutality of the Soviet forces, and the fact that many of its leaders were Jews, were directly responsible in significant measure for the great increase in the strength of the extreme right in inter-war Europe, and to the virulence of extreme anti-semitism, including Hitler and his world-view, a factor which is often overlooked by historians.

Churchill's anti-Bolshevism at this time emerged in large part from his conviction that Bolshevism, like Nazism fifteen years later, was 'beyond the pale' of Western civilisation at its furthest extremes, and represented a reversion to the anarchy, sadism, destruction, and senseless mass killings of the Reign of Terror in revolutionary France, only on a vastly greater and more dangerous scale. It also emerged from his broad and deep knowledge of history, a quality he shared with few other British politicians, and which helped him to understand Nazism.

Churchill's hostility towards Bolshevism was also a component of his general move to the right – indeed the far right – of British politics over the few years after 1919–22. By November 1924 Churchill was the *Tory* Chancellor of the Exchequer, an appointment inconceivable a few years earlier. The collapse of the Liberal party as the normal left-of-centre major party in Britain actually saw remarkably few other leading Liberal politicians reemerge as leading Tories. Indeed, probably the only other Liberal Cabinet minister of the 1905–16 Government to reemerge later as a leading Conservative was Sir John Simon (1873–1954), who sat as a Liberal Cabinet minister from 1913–16 and, in 1931–40, was a leading Cabinet minister in the National government, notorious in many circles for his strong support of Appeasement. Simon, however, was technically a Liberal National, that is, a Liberal ally of the Conservative-led National government who accepted the necessity for tariffs to alleviate the Depression. He was never, technically, a Conservative – unlike Churchill, who was officially a Conservative from 1924 on. Most of the surviving leading Liberals of the 1905–16 period who were active in politics, such as Asquith, Lloyd George, Herbert Samuel, and Lord Reading, remained loyal to the Liberals. A few, such as Christopher Addison (a Cabinet minister under Attlee) and Lord Haldane, joined the Labour party. Churchill's position was almost unique.

It is also important to note that Churchill did *not* remain a gung-ho, outspoken anti-Bolshevist after the early1920s, and, indeed, appears to have little to say about the subject until, in the late 1930s, he advocated an alliance *with* the Soviet Union to fight Nazism, which, as he specifically told Soviet Ambassador Ivan Maisky in 1938, presented a greater danger to Britain. (Robin Edmonds, "Churchill and

Stalin", in Robert Blake and William Roger Lewis, eds., *Churchill* (Oxford, 1996), p.311.) Of course, a few years later he would become a close ally of Stalin's, and then warn, after 1945, against Soviet expansionism in terms somewhat reminiscent, although less extreme, than his 1918–22 rhetoric. Whether he attacked Communism or Nazism, at all times Churchill was motivated by what he perceived as he greater threat to Western democracy, and especially to the English-speaking democracies.

Chapter Three

WINSTON CHURCHILL AND THE NAZIS

CHURCHILL IS, OF COURSE, MOST FAMOUS for his fierce opposition to Appeasement during the1930s and then for his indomitable war leadership which led to the utter defeat of Nazi Germany. We take it for granted that Churchill saw through Hitler from the first, and fought him virtually single-handedly among British politicians in the era of Appeasement. Because our common opinion of Churchill's prescient greatness at this time is so ingrained in our thinking, it is perhaps difficult to realise that it, too, is anomalous; perhaps highly anomalous. Churchill's attitude towards Nazi Germany represents, in a sense, the opposite side of the coin from his hostility, fifteen years earlier, to Bolshevism. By 1918–22 Churchill had established a long and genuine record as a senior politician of the centre-left. By1933, Churchill had also established an apparently genuine and widely perceived reputation as politician of the right, perhaps the far right, in particular over India. After losing office as Chancellor of the Exchequer in May 1929, Churchill became virtually obsessed with halting any moves towards Indian self-determination, as well as any moves towards withdrawal anywhere else in the Empire. The new minority Labour government moved swiftly towards trimming back some of Britain's imperial commitment. It announced plans to remove all British troops from Egypt apart the Suez Canal row, and recalled the British High Commissioner, Lord Lloyd. To these moves, Churchill reacted 'vehemently'. (Martin Gilbert,

Winston Churchill: The Wilderness Years (London, 1981), p.22.) Ramsay Macdonald's policy seemed also to have the support of Stanley Baldwin and the mainstream Tory leadership, to Churchill's chagrin. (*Ibid.*) In October 1929, the Labour government, through the Viceroy, Lord Irwin (later Lord Halifax), announced a new policy of Indian evolution whose final step would be 'the attainment of Dominion status' for the whole of India. (*Ibid.*, p.26.) Churchill immediately attacked this goal, especially because even semi-independent India would continue to brand the sixty million 'untouchables' as 'pollution'. (*Ibid.*) Vexatiously for Churchill, the aim of Dominion status for India appeared to have the full support of Stanley Baldwin, the Tory leader, as well as Lord Irwin, who had served in Tory Cabinets before becoming Viceroy, and of some of the Tory Front Bench – although at least one-third of Conservative M.P.s were opposed to it. Many of the future progenitors of Appeasement, such as Sir Samuel Hoare, also supported it, as did the *Times* and the BBC's Director General Sir John Reith (*Ibid.*, p.27). The clash between Churchill and Baldwin over this, and a number of other issues, led to Churchill's increasing alienation from most of the Tory Shadow Cabinet, of which he was still a member. In early 1931 a 'Round Table' Conference was held in London, at which the British government promised eventual Indian self-government, but one in which Britain would retain power over India's defence, foreign affairs, and army, and would guarantee the rights of all minorities. (*Ibid.*, p.32.) Baldwin immediately promised to support this new policy. Churchill now began in earnest a long campaign against Indian self-government and against the new official Tory policy. He also was resolute in his condemnation of Macdonld's 1929–31 Labour government, attacking a rage of its policies, including disarmament and the unrealistic near-pacifism pursued by the government. It was at this time that Churchill made two his most extreme and memorable attacking speeches. In Parliament in January 1931 Churchill attacked Macdonald by recalling that as child he had been taken by his parents to see a 'freak show' at Barnum's Circus, but that his parents had not allowed him to see 'the Boneless Wonder' as 'too revolting'. 'I have waited fifty years to see the boneless wonder sitting on the Treasury Bench', referring to the Prime Minister (*Ibid.*, p.33). The following month, when Lord Irwin met Gandhi in Delhi, Churchill made his famous attack on the meeting in a speech to the West Essex Conservative Association. 'It is alarming, and nauseating to see Mr. Gandhi, a seditious Middle Temple lawyer, now posing as a fakir of a type well-known in the East, standing half naked up the steps of the Viceregal palace … to parlay on equal terms with the representative of the King-Emperor.' (*Ibid.*, p.34. That Gandhi was indeed an English barrister is perhaps not as widely known as it might be.)

It was sentiments like this, frankly expressed, and, while aimed at Labour, also attacked the Conservative party's mainstream policies under Stanley Baldwin, which probably caused him to be excluded from the National Government when it was formed in August 1931. Churchill (and Lloyd George, who was ill) were probably the most important politicians deliberately excluded from the Government when it was formed by Ramsay Macdonald. Four Tories were included in the original National Cabinet after (Baldwin, Neville Chamberlain, Sir Samuel Hoare, and Sir Philip Cunliffe-Lister), along with a range of Tory junior ministers such as the young Anthony Eden. As the 1930s proceeded, the 'National' government became a nakedly Tory government, with the continuing admixture of a tiny number of 'National Labour' M.P.s and a larger group of 'Liberal Nationals', headed by Sir John Simon, who now accepted tariffs, but Churchill continued to be excluded. Only a handful of prominent Tories were continuously excluded from the National government, the most notable being Leopold Amery, who, like Churchill, was perceived as an extreme anti-Labour pro-Imperialist, disliked by Macdonald and mistrusted by some mainstream Tories. Also excluded were 'die hard' Tory backbenchers not of the first rank, such as Sir Henry Page Croft and John Gretton. Macdonald and Baldwin both preferred moderate, accommodating Tories and their allies, most of whom became arch-Appeasers later in the decade. Curiously, perhaps, the biggest Appeaser of all, Neville Chamberlain, was, like Churchill fiercely anti-Labour and detested by the Labour opposition. Chamberlain's economic, and administrative competence, progressive views on many aspects of social reform, and active business links meant that he served continuously in the National government, briefly as Minister of Health (August-November 1931 – May 1937), and then (May 1937 – May 1940) as perhaps the most controversial of all Prime Ministers.

Churchill, in contrast, was seen as an irresponsible and aggressive extremist, a romantic with great gifts but little practical sense, despite the many years he had served as a minister since 1905. He did manage to attract a handful of intensely loyal supporters, most notably Brendan Bracken, Professor Frederick Lindemann, Robert Boothby, but was generally perceived as a inflammatory *right wing* extremist. It is thus Churchill's *right* wing attitudes on the range of issues of the day, most importantly the Empire, which arguably makes his immediate hostility to Hitler and Nazism arguably anomalous, especially given his fierce anti-Bolshevism. Many right-wingers viewed Hitler, if too brutal and extreme, as a bulwark against Communism, who restored order and prosperity to Germany. Even many liberals – indeed, most if not all liberals –regarded his attempts to incorporate the German-speaking areas of central Europe in the Reich, in order to right the injustices of the Versailles Treaty, as at least arguably meritorious. Indeed, as will be seen, perceptions of the apparent reasonableness of Hitler's case, whatever the obvious brutality and loathsomeness of Nazi policy, was arguably the most important single element in the popularity of Appeasement. Churchill was one of a handful of politicians who rejected this viewpoint from the early days of the Nazi regime, most of the others were on the left, not the far right.

Churchill's hostility to Nazism was based in two underlying principles, his belief that German expansionism upset the European balance of power, and his hatred of Nazi totalitarianism and brutality. Churchill's opposition to any hint of German reemergence as a military power began *before* Hitler came to power. In September 1932 Churchill supported British Foreign Minister Sir John Simon's opposition to German minister Kurt von Schleicher's proposal that Germany rearm. (*Ibid.*, p.53.) Two months later, in a newspaper article – again before Hitler came to power – he attacked Germany's request for equal status in armaments. 'All these bands of sturdy Teutonic youths, marching through he streets and roads of Germany ... are not looking for [equal] status. They are looking for weapons ... for the return of lost territories and lost colonies ... [a] demand which will shatter to the foundations ... France, Belgium, Poland, Rumania, Czechoslovakia, and Yugoslavia,' he wrote, with uncanny prescience. (*Ibid.*, p.55.) In April 1933, he claimed that 'the rise of Germany to anything like military equality with France, Poland, or the small states, means the renewal of a general European war,' more than six years before it actually broke out. (*Ibid.*, p.62.) In September 1935 a French woman who met Churchill during his summer holiday at Cannes attached his criticism of Italy's invasion of

Abyssinia, claiming that England had done much the same thing in the Empire. 'Ah,' Churchill replied, 'all that is locked away in the limbo of the old, wicked days. The world progresses. We have endeavoured, by means of the League of Nations, ... to make it impossible for nations nowadays to infringe on each others rights ... who is to say what will come of it in a year, or two, or three? With Germany arming at breakneck speed, England lost in a pacifist dream, France corrupt and torn by dissention, America remote and indifferent –Madame, my dear lady, do you not tremble for your children?' (*Ibid.*, p.130.) Countless other statements by Churchill during the 1930s demonstrating his belief in collective European security, headed by Britain, as the only way to stop the emergence of a European hegemon, can be readily found.

Churchill's belief in the necessity for Britain to maintain the European balance of power as the basis for general peace and security is, paradoxically, perhaps the least original and most derivative component of his foreign policy agenda during the period. Maintenance of the European balance of power had been the absolute cornerstone of Britain's foreign policy towards Europe from the time of the Spanish Armada to, arguably, the end of the Cold War. In most times, it had been universally supported by the entire British political mainstream, both the left and the right, and was the centre of a policy aimed over the centuries at kings, emperors, and dictators. Yet, from 1933 until 1939, it was a policy which, almost uniquely in history, seemed extremist and pointlessly provocative.

The reason for this is that the pro-Appeasers in Britain were, almost uniquely, prepared to abandon the maintenance of the balance of power in Europe as the keystone of British policy *provided that* Hitler's goals were limited and seemingly reasonable. It is this consideration which was at the heart of the case made by Neville Chamberlain and his associates in favour of Appeasement. There were other arguments, but this was the principal one. Hitler –it seemed to many until March 1939 – was merely bent on reunifying the German-speaking areas of central Europe into a united German *Reich*. However brutal his methods, and however horrifying his dictatorship at home, so long as Hitler seemed to be solely aiming at the limited goal of bringing German-speaking territory into Germany, his actions seemed both limited and manageable, and even justified. Hitler's argument – if that is the right term – is that the Wilsonian settlement of 1918–19 enacted at Versailles made nationality – which formerly meant the language spoken there – the basis of European national boundaries. This was applied in favour of Poland, Austria, Hungary, Romania, etc., but was palpably and deliberately not applied to Germany, whose 1918–19 boundaries excluded Austria, the Sudetenland (chiefly composed of German speakers) and border areas in Poland such as Danzig. This principle was not applied to Germany solely because it was being punished for losing the war. What Hitler intended to do – as he publicly stated very often – was merely to reunite these areas with Germany, thus correcting the injustice of Versailles. At that point, he often said that he would stop. Indeed, under

Nazi racialist theory, it seemed a contradiction for Hitler to attempt to gain millions of Slavic and Jewish subjects in non-Germanic areas of Europe. At this point, Hitler's aims *vis-à-vis* the Jews was to expel them from Germany and the *Reich*, in order to create a racially pure Germany composed exclusively of 'Aryan Germans'.

If Hitler could be appeased by accepting an enlarged, but purely 'Aryan' Germany, at which his point his 'territorial demands' would cease, it seemed to Chamberlain and his allies that Britain and France should accede to his demands, however terrible the Nazi regime, in preference to starting an European war in which millions would be killed and Bolshevism the probably only winner. For Britain to arm for a war, unless it had no other option, also threatened its economic prosperity, while any highly visible policy of rearmament would, in and of itself, be interpreted by Germany (and Italy) as an aggressive act. But prior to any concerted programme of rearmament, Britain simply lacked the military force necessary to defeat

Germany in a war. France, its only reliable Great Power ally, was politically divided and oriented almost wholly around a defensive policy based on the Maginot Line. Britain had only two other potential Great Power allies, the Soviet Union, itself an unimaginably brutal, ideologically motivated dictatorship whose purges made it unreliable and weak, and the United States, at this stage wholly isolationist and virtually disarmed. For all of these reasons, it was far better for Britain to pursue a policy of Appeasement, hoping that Germany would stop once German-speaking Europe was absorbed, and in the meantime increasing its military capacity and its alliance with France. Realistically, it had few other options. Conceivably, Italy under Mussolini could be detached from supporting Nazi Germany (as seemed possible to many), but the cost of this would be to allow Mussolini to create a Mediterranean and African empire, threatening British interests. An alliance with Stalin was also at least possible, but Stalin's great purge of his military officers came at just the time (1937–38) when a strong Soviet military was most necessary. In any case, the Soviet Union had no common boundary with Czechoslovakia, and could only intervene militarily there if allowed to march through Poland or Romania, to which neither country would ever agree; in any case, too, Stalin would obviously try to impose pro Bolshevik governments wherever he went. For all of these pressing and unpalatable reasons, Appeasement was the only possible course for Britain to pursue, and one which held out the seemingly realistic chance that it would prevent a new World War. Since Hitler's demands for the reunification of German territories seemed just to many liberals, if Appeasement failed, it would bring a wholly united British nation into the War, as even liberals and leftists could not argue that a less hostile policy towards Germany might have prevented a European war.

These are powerful and perhaps compelling arguments, and seemed so to *most* British politicians and opinion-makers until March 1939. In March 1939 Germany occupied the rump of the Czech state (Bohemia and Moravia), the first time that a non-Germanic area had been taken over by Hitler, and evidence that he was bent, not merely on unifying German-speaking Europe, but on dominating the entire Continent. Hitler's seizure of Bohemia-Moravia led to a fundamental reassessment of British policy, with Chamberlain reversing his former stance, and offering (for the first time) military alliance pacts with other potentially threatened European states, including Poland. It was the pact made by Britain (and France) with Poland at this time which, of course, directly led to the outbreak of the Second World War.

Churchill's alternative policy, based in the strict legality and permanent status of the Versailles settlement, and founded in Britain's centuries old support for the maintenance of the European Balance of Power as its basis, emerged as prescient after March 1939. During and after the War, it received the endorsement of most commentators and historians, including his own highly influential *War Memoirs*. It was only in the 1960s that Appeasement again came to be given the benefit of the doubt by historians. (On the evolution attitudes towards British foreign policy in the 1930s, see the excellent summary in Robert J. Caputi, *Neville Chamberlain and Appeasement* (Cranbury, N.J., 2000).) But acceptance of the normal highly critical view of Appeasement is based entirely in its failure, a failure which was not evident in March 1939 or even later. This ambiguity was in large measure a deliberate contrivance by Hitler himself, who appeared to hold both the limited and manageable aims of the reunification of German speakers, while also, especially in private, harbouring well-advanced intentions of pan-European domination. Churchill – and only a few others – saw through the smokescreen of moderation in which Hitler enveloped himself.

By upholding the traditional view of Britain's primary role as maintaining the Balance of Power in Europe, ironically Churchill was supporting the long-established view of British policy, while the Appeasers were advocating a radical break with British policy, and an acquiescence in a vast expansion of German power in central Europe, *even if* Hitler did not begin a war. That Chamberlain's policies marked a sharp break with those perceived by all British governments from the time of Queen Elizabeth and the Spanish Armada does not appear to have attracted much attention from either his contemporaries or subsequent historians. This sharp break with time-honoured policy, in the face of a grave, violent, and barbaric threat of widespread conquest by a palpable madman, is not the least objectionable aspect of Appeasement.

Churchill's anti-Appeasement stance thus had several separate but interrelated prongs to it: specific hostility to brutal Nazi totalitarianism; hostility to European totalitarianism *per se* and support for Anglo-American democracy; and a determination to uphold the traditional British policy of maintaining the Balance of Power in Europe. It had several subsidiary aspects as well: a desire to maintain the power and integrity of the British Empire, which would obviously be threatened in the Middle East, India, and the Far East, by expansionist fascist powers; and a general distrust of the mediocrity and complacency of interwar British politics, especially under Stanley Baldwin, in comparison with the sharper and more 'heroic' politics of the Edwardian era, with its larger than life leading figures. The perception that the British Empire was threatened by fascism, and despite Churchill's central hostility to any concessions to Indian independence, was not in fact a central component of his anti-Appeasement stance in the later 1930s. Churchill appears to have said little about India after the passage of the India Act of 1935. This was in contrast, for example, to Leopold Amery, an arch-imperialist and also, in the later 1930s, an arch anti-Appeaser, for whom maintenance of the Empire as a relatively unified bloc in world politics was paramount. Amery was long able to contemplate concessions to Nazi Germany in central Europe but was strenuously opposed to ceding back to Germany any of the colonies it lost in 1918, such as Tanganyika, as was widely suggested in the 1930s. (On which see Richard S. Grayson, 'Leo Amery's Imperialist Alternatives to Appeasement in the 1930s', *Twentieth*

Century British History, 17(4) (2007), pp.489–515.) Determining which of the strands in Churchill's anti-Appeasement views – his opposition to Nazi totalitarianism; his support for Anglo-American democracy; or his wish to maintain the traditional British 'Balance of Power' policy – was the most important is not entirely clear: each reinforced the other. *Probably*, however, his realisation of the extreme and unique evil presented by Hitler and Nazism was the most important. As with Bolshevism, Churchill saw quickly that Nazism was outside the Western mainstream at its widest limits, and that Hitler presented Europe, and Western democracy, with arguably the gravest threat in a thousand years. There seems no doubt that, as early as May 1934, Churchill had taken the wholly accurate measure of Nazism. In a magazine article Churchill published in May 1934, Churchill claimed that the German people 'the most powerful and the most dangerous in the world', had reverted to medieval barbarism 'with all the modern facilities and aggravations'. Nazi Germany represented 'the monstrosity of the totalitarian state' where any criticism of the regime was considered 'heresy and treason'. He also quickly realised the enormity of Nazi policy towards the Jews, even at that relatively early date. 'Jews must be baited for being born Jews', he continued, 'little Jewish children must be ... made to feel the ignominy of the state of life to which the Creator has called them.' Moreover, 'Venerable pastors, upright magistrates, world famous philosophers, capable statesman ... [and] frail old women ... are invaded, bullied and brutalised by gangs of armed hooligans, to resist whom is a capital offence.' (Cited in Gilbert, *Winston Churchill: The Wilderness Years* (*op.cit.*, p.111.) The following year, in another article published in the *Strand* magazine, Churchill enlarged on these themes:

The twentieth century has witnessed with surprise, not merely the promulgation of these ferocious doctrines, but their enforcement with brutal vigour by the Government and by the populace. No past services, no proved patriotism, even wounds sustained in war, could procure immunity for persons whose only crime was that their parents had brought them into the world. Every kind of persecution, grave or petty, upon the world-famous scientists, writers, composers at the top down to the wretched little Jewish children in the national schools, was practiced, was glorified, and is still being practiced and glorified.

In the same article, Churchill noted that 'a similar proscription fell upon socialists and communists of every hue [and on] the Trade Unionists and the liberal intelligentsia ...' (Quoted in Martin Gilbert, *Winston S. Churchill, Vol.5, 1922–1939* (London, 1976), p.681.)

While all of this appears commonplace and obvious to us today, this was not the case in the mid-1930s. Few in the Western democracies believed that the Nazis were as extreme as they seemed, or that their ferocious persecutions would last literally throughout the history of the Nazi regime until its last day, let alone that they could become unimaginably more horrible and be effected throughout Europe.

Churchill's early and unwavering belief that the Nazis were uniquely evil and had to be stopped, thus came from a variety of sources: his deep knowledge of history, especially of the evolution of Anglo-American democracy; his surprising – for someone who might also be described as a 'romantic' – realism and refusal to perceive a silver lining in a situation where there was none; his sympathy for the persecuted victims of the Nazis; and his commitment to a continuation of British maintenance of the Balance of Power as the central basis of its foreign policy in Europe.

Churchill's pro-Appeasement opponents, in contrast, refused to contemplate war in Europe except as a last resort; were willing to abandon the notion of the maintenance of the Balance of Power in Europe as the basis of British policy; viewed Nazi persecution of the Jews and others as no doubt horrible, but not necessarily the hallmark of a regime utterly beyond the pale of Western civilisation;

and, above all, saw the satisfaction of Germany's 'legitimate' territorial demands as the best way to avoid a major war, assuming that Hitler would stop once all the German-speaking areas of central Europe were incorporated into the *Reich*. As we have seen, there is arguably nothing unreasonable in this last assumption, and Hitler repeatedly sounded as if he would indeed stop any demands or aggression once his territorial demands were met. In the end, it was Churchill, rather than his pro-Appeasement opponents, who turned out to be absolutely correct. In the final analysis, it was Churchill's clear-headed understanding of totalitarianism, based in his wide and deep knowledge of history, which best explains this fact.

It must be said, however, that Churchill's across-the-board hatred of totalitarianism did not, at that time, always serve him in good stead. Churchill's deep and genuine hostility to Bolshevism, as R.A.C. Parker shows in his *Churchill and Appeasement* (London, 2000, esp. pp.138–166), made him very cool to any alliance with the Soviet Union until the very last minute, relying, instead, on the promise of a real military accord with France to halt German aggression, Churchill did swallow his hatred of the Soviet Union by the time of Munich (see Parker, pp.212–219), although very reluctantly. Not until he had been Prime Minister for over a year and the Soviet Union was attacked in June 1941 did he wholly repent. Within three years, however, he was again extremely wary of Soviet intentions, with good reason.

Chapter Four

CHURCHILL
AND THE
JEWS

A CHAPTER IN THIS WORK ON CHURCHILL
and the Jews may well seem out of place and
inappropriate. Ostensibly, Churchill had little or
no direct connection with the Jews. Despite this, at
least two books have been written on this subject –
Michael J. Cohen, *Churchill and the Jews* (London,
1985) and Martin Gilbert, *Churchill and the Jews*
(London, 2007) – with significantly different

viewpoints. Both agree that Churchill was a lifelong philo-semite and pro-Zionist. Although not perhaps extremely uncommon, Churchill's stance, lasting a lifetime, among men of his class background, and with few direct Jewish connections, is rather unusual. Given Churchill's move from the left to the right of British politics after 1918, it is arguably very unusual, for Churchill absorbed almost nothing of the casual anti-semitism of the British upper classes.

To be sure, Churchill in elected office impinged directly on Jewish affairs only on a handful of occasions. He was a newly-appointed Liberal M.P. in 1905 when the Aliens Act was passed. He was Minister of Munitions, and a Cabinet Minister, in November 1917 when the Balfour Declaration was promulgated. He was Colonial Secretary in 1921–22 when significant changes in the nature of the Palestine Mandate were enacted while he was Minister. He was Prime Minister from 1940 to 1945, when the Holocaust occurred. He was again Prime Minister from 1951 to 1955, when there was an armed peace in the Arab-Israeli conflict. None of the many other official positions held by Churchill in his long career directly impacted on the Jews or a Jewish question, although as the main opponent of Nazi expansionism and of Appeasement in the 1930s he was motivated in part by a deep loathing of Nazi anti-semitism. He was also leader of the Opposition from 1945 until 1951, during the controversial period of British hostility to Zionism, of the creation of the State of Israel, and the Israeli War of Independence, but of course played no role in formulating British policy, and had a plethora of other concerns. Nevertheless, Churchill's stance towards the Jews formed a distinctive and arguably consistent component of his long career.

Churchill had no Jewish ancestry or relatives. (Claims that his mother Jenny Jerome was of Jewish descent are entirely false.) During his long life, Churchill had surprisingly few close friends or long-term associates, and only a few close Jewish friends. The most important of these was his American friend and confidant Bernard Baruch (1879–1965), one of the preeminent *eminent grises* of American public life for nearly as long as Churchill himself. Baruch was, unusually for a prominent American Jew, born in South Carolina. His father, a German immigrant who became a doctor, was a surgeon on the staff of Confederate General Robert E. Lee during the Civil War. His Sephardic mother came from New York, where Baruch lived after 1881. Baruch made a fortune as the 'lone wolf of Wall Street' and a prominent stockbroker. During the First World War he was appointed by President Wilson as Chairman of the War Industries Board, the virtual czar of America's wartime production. Churchill, who was Minister of Munitions from July 1917 until January 1919 (surely the least-known Cabinet post Churchill ever held) exchanged many messages with him, although he apparently did not meet him until after the War. From then on, Baruch became probably Churchill's closest American friend. It was when attempting to find Baruch's New York apartment in December 1931 that Churchill, forgetting he was in America, famously got out of the wrong side of the taxi he was riding, was almost killed and spend eight days in hospital. (Martin Gilbert, *Churchill and America*

(London, 2005), pp.130–133.) Baruch represented the kind of fiercely independent, highly intelligent, self-made personality that Churchill often admired. Although Baruch was Jewish, well-known to be Jewish, and kept up the main Jewish holidays, he did not act in any way as a spokesman for the Jewish community and married a Protestant. Churchill and Baruch remained friends until the end of their lives, which occurred within a few months of each other. Churchill's other apparently close Jewish friend was the English Tory M.P. Sir Philip Sassoon, 2nd Bt. (1888–1939), the scion of the phenomenally wealthy Sephardic family. The Etonian Sassoon, who had been Sir Douglas Haig's private secretary during the First World War and was a Tory minister between 1934 and his premature death, owned several fabulous country houses at which Churchill was a guest. Nevertheless, this is a very short list. Churchill had few intimate friends, either as cronies (like F.E. Smith) whom he treated as equals, as admiring epigones (like Brendan Bracken or Robert Boothby) who had attached themselves to him; or as technical advisors (like Professor Frederick Lindemann, later

Lord Cherwell, Churchill's scientific advisor, who, despite his name, was of 'Aryan' German descent), of whom only a handful were Jewish. He did, until the association of Lord Moyne in 1944, frequently speak with Chaim Weizmann, the leader of the Zionist movement, who was a reader in chemistry at Manchester University, and to other Jewish leaders, but he was not really close to them. In his *Churchill and the Jews* (p.308), Sir Martin Gilbert made a point of noting Churchill's apparently frequent contact with Jews: 'A Jewish banker was his patron after the early death of his father. A Jewish refugee from Hitler was his European literary agent. A leading Jewish historian gave him advice on his biography of his ancestor John Churchill, Duke of Marlborough. A young Jewish philosopher was among his small team of researchers on his four-volume *A History of the English-Speaking Peoples*. One of his favourite sculptors was a Jew.' (The references here are, it seems, respectively, to Sir Ernest Cassel, Emery Reves, Sir Lewis Namier, Sir Isaiah Berlin or Sir Maurice Shock, and Oscar Neuman.) Yet with none of these, with the possible exception of Reves (1904–81), a Hungarian born Jew who migrated to England around 1933 and became Churchill's literary agent in 1937, was Churchill really close. Churchill had many Jewish friends and acquaintances, but arguably none with whom he was intimate. Churchill appears to have had few Jews prominently on his staff (unlike, say, Ramsay Macdonald, whose private secretary, Rose Rosenberg, was Jewish) or as assistants in his historical research or writing ventures. (An exception was Sir Maurice Shock, a literary assistant in 1956–57. Sir Martin Gilbert (1936–2015), his official biographer, who was Jewish, had no contact with Churchill in his lifetime.) Neither his 1945 'Caretaker' Tory Cabinet nor his 1951–55 peacetime Tory Cabinet contained any professing Jews, although the former included two men, Leopold Amery and the sixth Earl of Rosebery, whose mothers were Jewish. Churchill may or may not have been aware of Amery's background, which he kept very quiet if not secret during his lifetime, although he certainly knew that Rosebery was the offspring of Lord Rosebery the Prime Minister and Hannah

Rothschild, the principal Rothschild heiress of her day. Churchill and Amery were at Harrow at the same time (where Amery pushed Churchill into a swimming pool), but, despite the general similarity of their pro-imperialist outlooks, managed to be on opposite sides in most of the major political controversies between Chamberlain's Tariff Reform proposals in 1903 and the battle over Indian self-determination in the mid-1930s. Churchill thus appears to have been personally friendly towards Jews, and had had his share of Jewish associates, although in truth probably no more than anyone in the British upper classes and a famous politician and author for over sixty years, is likely to have had. Considering the centrality of his anti-Hitler stance, pursued virtually alone in the mid-1930s, to his place in British history, it is actually striking how few were his direct contacts with Jews or how few were among those who influenced him. Yet, despite this, he was a lifelong philo-semite and pro-Zionist, often when, as it were, there was no logical reason for him to be either.

Churchill's father and mother were both friendly with wealthy Jews, especially Nathaniel, first Baron Rothschild, Sir Ernest Cassel, and Baron Maurice de Hirsch. (Gilbert, *Churchill and the Jews*, pp.2–3.) This is at least slightly unusual. One assumes that upper class British aristocrats – Lord Randolph Churchill, Winston's father, was of course the son of the Duke of Marlborough – and, more emphatically, self-made W.A.S.P. American millionaires of the time and their families, such as Jenny Jerome's background, would have been at least mildly anti-semitic, especially in social situations. However, this is only a negative stereotype, an unproven supposition, while, in any case, money almost always speaks a multi-cultural language. Churchill's doctor, Sir Felix Semon, who attempted to cure his slight speech defect, was also Jewish, and Churchill was a convinced pro-Dreyfusard, deploring the unfair, anti-semitic persecution of the French army officer. (Gilbert, *Ibid.*, p.3.) The latter point is not as surprising as it might seem: *most* Establishment figures in Britain supported Dreyfus. The anti-semitic writer Hilaire Belloc, who was an undergraduate at the time, always claimed that he was the only anti-Dreyfusard at Oxford, and was denied a fellowship at All Souls for that reason. Nor should it be forgotten that Churchill was moving irresistibly to the political Liberalism which would mark his career from about 1903 until 1924. British Liberalism had religious tolerance and the right of minorities at its heart, although occasionally (as with its anti-Disraeli agitation during the time of the 'Bulgarian atrocities' of 1878–80), its leaders, heavily influenced by Evangelical Christianity, could engage in a hint of anti-semitism.

Churchill's first close encounter with Jews came in 1904–6, when, although an elected Tory M.P., he became the Liberal candidate for Manchester North-West, where one-third of the electorate was Jewish. At this time he strongly opposed the Aliens Act, which limited Jewish immigration to Britain, and became a supporter of Zionism. His support for Zionism was mainly as a result of his contact with Chaim Weizmann, the leader of the Zionist movement in Britain (and, from 1949 until 1952, the first President of Israel), who was a lecturer in chemistry at Manchester University. Manchester was then emerging as possibly the main locus of Zionism in Britain, and was also the home of the Marks and Sieff families of Marks and Spencers, possibly the greatest financial backers of the Zionist movement, and later of Sir Lewis Namier, the great historian and Zionist intellectual. Churchill became a lifelong supporter of Zionism at that time, and also personally gave generously to many local Jewish charities (Gilbert, *op.cit.*, p.14) – of course, what one might expect of a candidate for Parliament, but Churchill was apparently a sincere admirer of the Jewish community, and never lost an opportunity to defend it from attack. During the First World War, Churchill supported the Balfour Declaration, promulgated in October 1917 (when he was in the Cabinet as Minister of Munitions) and continued to support it, albeit sometimes controversially. In 1920–21, now as Colonial Secretary, Churchill took the controversial decision to set the boundaries of the Palestine Mandate at the familiar borders, its eastern boundary being the Jordan River and

Red Sea, and excluding what is now the kingdom of Jordan, east of the River Jordan, where Jewish immigration would be prohibited. This conflicted with the desire of the Zionist movement for a considerable portion of the western part of what is now Jordan to be included in the areas assigned to the Jews. As compensation, he included the Negev area in the Jewish territory. (Gilbert, *Churchill*, *op.cit.*, pp.48–50.) Churchill's boundaries persisted until 1948, and, even today, define the extent of Israel and the Palestinian territories. By defining these boundaries to reflect natural frontiers, they probably brought a measure of stability, as well as appeasing radical Arab opinion. They also ensured that a Jewish proto-state would exist in some form, recognised by the British government.

On 8 February 1920 Churchill produced one of his most curious pieces of journalism on the Jews, and one which has given rise to much debate and perhaps misunderstanding ever since. His 'Zionism Versus Bolshevism / A Struggle for the Soul of the Jewish People' appeared in the *Illustrated Sunday Herald*.

Churchill began remarkably by paying unexpected tribute to the Jews as 'beyond all question the most formidable and the most remarkable race which has ever appeared in the world.' He then divided Jews between good Jews and bad Jews – a dichotomy which was voiced over and over again at that time and later. Among the former were 'national Jews', the patriots of the democracies. Among the latter were the 'International Jews', which he termed 'a sinister confederacy' stretching 'from the days of Spartacus-Weishaupt to those of Karl Marx, and from Lenin to Trotsky (Russia), Bela Kun (Hungary), Rosa Luxemburg (Germany), and Emma Goldman (United States), [a] world-wide conspiracy for the overthrow of civilisation.' His language was obviously painful, in light of subsequent events, but Churchill then goes on to make a wholly unexpected further crucial point, namely that Western gentiles ought to support Zionism and the idea of a Jewish National Home as the only 'positive and practical alternative' to Jewish support for Bolshevism: the gentile West should be engaged 'in building up with the utmost possible rapidity a Jewish national

centre in Palestine which may become not only a
refuge to the oppressed from the unhappy lands
of Central Europe, but which will also be a symbol
of Jewish unity and the temple of Jewish glory ...'
Churchill's central argument, that Zionism was the
only realistic counterweight to Jewish Bolshevism,
was extraordinarily original for a gentile British
politician. It was however, one which would have
been fully endorsed by Jewish nationalistic right-
wing Zionists such as Vladimir Jabotinsky, the
founder of what became the Likud party in Israel.
It was also remarkably prescient: formerly almost
always classified as a 'people of the left', since 1967
or so many Jews have moved to the right of the
political spectrum as Israeli policy and even its
legitimacy has been questioned by the Western left,
while virtually all Jews have long since abandoned
support for Bolshevism or radical movements.
Jewish nationalism has been, in fact, a realistic and
successful counterweight to Jewish radicalism, a
point Churchill saw with amazing clarity in 1920.
His view that it was altogether in the interests of
Western conservatives to support Zionism has also,

equally, been endorsed by history, with the State of Israel now a Western, pro-American bastion in the Middle East.

During the 1930s, outrage at Nazi treatment of the Jews – as evidence in some of the quotes noted in the previous chapter – was an important part of Churchill's motivation in opposing Appeasement and denouncing Nazi Germany. He did this without pointed urging by Jewish sources (although he was supported, financially and in other ways, by Jewish and also Czech bodies), and as a major component, but certainly not the only one, in Churchill's gut hatred of Nazi Germany and Hitler. As a result of Churchill's resolute stance against Nazism, he was and is viewed (along with President Franklin Roosevelt) as one of the greatest friends of the Jews, although many Jewish commentators are also critical of aspects of Churchill's stance, especially of his failure to rescue more European Jews from the Nazis, and his failure, in wartime, to create a Jewish state in Palestine.

CHURCHILL: THE CONTRADICTIONS OF GREATNESS

Probably the most controversial aspect of Churchill's policy towards the Jews occurred during the Holocaust. Churchill did little to rescue Jews. Churchill's lack of action has been questioned by recent historians critical of the Allies' response to the Holocaust, and, among specialist historians of this subject, by Michael J. Cohen, in *Churchill and the Jews* (*op.cit.*, pp.261–3054). One characteristic of Churchill's critics is that they habitually decline to say what precisely Churchill should have done, apart from bombing Auschwitz. The claim that more Jewish refugees should have been admitted to Britain is logically unsound, since (as this author has pointed out at length in *The Myth of Rescue: Why the Democracies Could Not Have Rescued More Jews from the Nazis* (1997)) the Jews of Nazi-occupied Europe were, after 1940–41, no longer refugees as they had been in the 1930s – but the exact opposite, prisoners of Hitler who were forbidden to leave.

The alleged failure of Churchill to 'do more' thus runs up immediately against the very real objection that there was nothing, realistically, that the Allies could do to rescue the Jews of Nazi-occupied Europe apart from winning the War and liberating Europe, which they were in the process of doing. The Jews of Nazi-occupied Europe were, tragically, absolutely at the mercy of Hitler and beyond the Allies' reach, certainly for most of the War. This issue is also bedevilled by the fact that *most* Jewish groups in the West used the War to demand the immediate or very rapid creation of a Jewish state in Palestine. Leaving either the realism or the propriety of this demand aside – which was certain to alienate millions of Arabs – the creation of a Jewish state would not have saved or rescue any Jews in Nazi-occupied Europe, who were, as noted, prisoners of Hitler in the process of being systematically murdered. Indeed, Zionist groups appear to have focussed on this aim precisely because they could not rescue any Jews.

Churchill (along with Roosevelt) has also been heavily criticised for failing to bomb Auschwitz. The story here is also more complicated than is often thought. No one, anywhere, proposed bombing

Auschwitz, or the railway lines to Auschwitz, or any other concentration camp until April or May 1944, when Rabbi Michael Dov Weissmandl (1903–57) escaped from a transport to Auschwitz, made his way to Slovakia, and managed to send messages to emissaries in the West proposing the bombing of one railway line from Hungary to Auschwitz. This had never been proposed before by anyone, and appears in no plan for the rescue of Jews made previously. It was initially greeted with a lack of enthusiasm by Jewish groups, as likely to kill Jews without ending the killing process. The U.S. War Refugee Board, created specifically to rescue Jews from the Holocaust, refused officially to endorse the bombing proposal until October 1944, a few weeks before the gassings ended. The proposal would also have diverted aircraft at precisely the time of the preparations for D-Day and the actual Normandy landings, on which the fate of the War depended. It is very doubtful if the bombing technology existed in 1944 to destroy Auschwitz's gas chambers, the size of a tennis court, from bombs dropped by Allied bombers of the time. (See my *The Myth of Rescue*, *op.cit.*, pp.1157–181.) In the last volume (six) of his *The Second World War* (p.597), Churchill described the Holocaust as 'probably the greatest and most horrible crime ever committed in the whole history of the world.'

Churchill's stance on Zionism and the creation of a Jewish state in Palestine should also be seen in a wider context. Churchill could not simply create a Jewish state in Palestine in war time without crucially offending the Arabs to the point of open revolt, which, plainly, no sane British government would have done. That a Jewish state should have been created during the War is also a *non sequitur* to the question of rescuing Jews from the Nazis, since, as noted, the central obstacle to the rescue of Jews was not that they had nowhere to flee, but that they were forbidden to leave. Moreover, the Zionist movement was never officially committed to the creation of an independent Jewish state in Palestine (as opposed to a vaguer 'homeland') until the so-called Biltmore Declaration of 1942, while, even then, Jewish opinion around the world was often still surprisingly hostile to Zionism. Churchill's stance was also influenced by the assassination in Cairo in November 1944 of Lord Moyne, his friend, by Zionist terrorists from the Stern Gang. Churchill apparently never met with Chaim Weizmann again, although he continued to enthusiastically support Zionism. He was, of course, in opposition when Israel was created in 1948 and during the immediately preceding period of terrorism and bloodshed in Palestine. Later, after Israel had been created, he stated on many occasions his support for Israel and Zionism. In 1952, for instance, he noted in an Address to the American Congress, 'From the days of the Balfour Declaration I have desired that the Jews should have a National Home, and I have worked for that end. I rejoice to pay any tribute here to the achievements of those who have founded the Israelite (*sic*) State, who have defended themselves with tenacity, and who offer asylum to great numbers of Jewish refugees.' Gilbert documents (*op.cit.*, pp.280–306) literally dozens of similar statements that Churchill made in the last decades of his life, after Israeli independence had been achieved.

Despite some apparent lapses, Churchill's consistent philo-semitism and pro-Zionism over a sixty year period is remarkable and, as with so much of his career, quite anomalous for a politician of his background and orientation.

Churchill's stance on the Jews, Zionism, and the establishment of the State of Israel might usefully be contrasted with that of Clement Attlee and many of the leaders of the Labour Party just after the Second World War. All Labourites were, of course, fiercely anti-Nazi and were all well aware of the Holocaust and of the unparalleled atrocities carried out by Hitler and the Nazi regime. Although Churchill had been appalled by the assassination of his friend Lord Moyne, the British Minister Resident in the Middle East, by Zionist terrorists in Cairo in November 1944, an act which weakened somewhat his support for the creation of the Jewish state, he remained more sympathetic to Zionism than were Attlee and Ernest Bevin, Attlee's Foreign Minister.

Both have been accused of overt anti-semitism, with Hugh Dalton (Attlee's first Chancellor of the Exchequer) claiming that Attlee excluded two Jewish backbench Labour M.P.s, Austen Albu and Ian Mikardo, from holding posts in the Labour government (as Dalton remembered Attlee's words) "because they belonged to the Chosen People and he didn't think he wanted any more of them." Attlee also described Zionism in a 1946 letter to his brother Tom as "a profitable racket. A Zionist is defined as a Jew who collects money from another Jew to send money to Palestine," a sentiment more likely today to be found on an extremist anti-semitic website than espoused by Britain's Prime Minister. (Leo McKinistry, *Attlee and Churchill: Allies in War, Adversaries in Peace* (London 2019), pp. 475–6.) The lack of sympathy for Zionism by Attlee (and also by Ernest Bevin) appears to foreshadow the anti-Zionism of the Labour party's left wing seventy years later, with Jeremy Corbyn and the "Corbynistas" demonstrating a deep hostility towards Israel and support for its enemies which has been widely seen as crossing the line to anti-semitism. And again in contrast, Churchill's relative warmth towards Zionism seems to have been a forerunner to the strong support shown today by most of the Western world's conservative leaders, political parties, and media advocates.

Chapter Five

CHURCHILL, THE EMPIRE AND THE UNITED STATES

AS WE HAVE SEEN, PROTECTING THE EMPIRE from independence and self-determination at the time when Indian Dominion status was being urged was one of Churchill's great aims, and highly significant in his move to the far right of politics. In November 1942 Churchill famously declared in a speech at the Mansion House that 'I have not become the King's first Minister in order to preside over the liquidation of the British Empire', a remark which is often quoted to summarise his attitude towards British Imperialism. Yet, paradoxically, beside Churchill's support for the Empire was an even deeper and arguably more important advocacy of a position even more basic to his world-view, his support for the Anglo-American alliance and the unity of the English-speaking world as the basis for democratic world hegemony. As some recent historians have noted, these two positions were in part incompatible, leading to Churchill's willingness to surrender many of Britain's assets and much of its power to American hegemony during the Second World War. It was also a relatively original position for any British politician to hold at the time, and is, again, evidence of the highly original nature of Churchill's outlook.

The origins of Churchill's Anglo-Imperial-American outlook presumably lie in his background as the product of a British father from a ducal family and an American mother from *nouveau riche* business origins. Although the key to Churchill's outlook almost certainly lies in his personal background, and although it was relatively unusual, it was not unique. Many leading British politicians had close American connections. Joseph Chamberlain's third wife was an American. The wife of Lord Curzon, synonymous with aristocratic *hauteur*, was the daughter of a Chicago meat-packing millionaire who had made a fortune in the Chicago stockyards. Charles Stewart Parnell's mother was an American, so, too, were the mothers of Harold Macmillan and Quintin Hogg (Lord Hailsham of St. Marylebone), and doubtless many other British politicians had American connections, while Andrew Bonar Law and Lord Beaverbrook were Canadians. None of these came close to duplicating Churchill's unique Anglo-American ideological blend, Chamberlain, Curzon, and Beaverbrook for instance, were arch-Imperialists who had no apparent special love for the United States.

Churchill's penchant for viewing history in terms of an Anglo-American alliance, with the United States seen as simply a transatlantic outpost of the same hegemonic English-speaking peoples, was highly original and probably arose from, his unusually wide and deep knowledge of history. If Churchill was practically unique in anything, it was in his genuinely deep historical knowledge and learning, which went far beyond any of his political contemporaries, the Fabian socialists possible excepted. In this, Churchill – if the point will not seem an insult – resembled those other twentieth-century political auto-didacts, Hitler and Stalin, who were both voracious readers with a wide and deep (and precise) knowledge of history.

Churchill's attitude towards the British Empire was itself rather complex. For the white Dominions, he favoured self-government. In South Africa in 1906– 07, as the Under-Secretary in the Colonial Office, he was one of the leaders of granting the maximum degree of self-government to the former Boer republics within what, in 1910, became the Union of South Africa, despite his own role as a soldier in the recent Boer War. (See, for instance, Roy Jenkins, *Churchill* (2001), pp.113–120.) Throughout his long career, however, Churchill had a tendency to take the white Dominions for granted, hardly ever including them within his world-view, except as marginal attachments to Britain. In Australia, for instance, Churchill is often not highly regarded, given his role in instituting the poorly conceived Gallipoli campaign, at which so many Australian and New Zealand troops lost their lives, and because of his relative neglect of Australian security during the Second World War, with the terrible loss of Singapore in February 1942, leaving the way open for an actual Japanese invasion of Australia. As a result, Australian Prime Minister John Curtin famously reoriented Australian foreign policy to view America as the country's 'great and powerful friend', in place of Britain. Similarly, perhaps, Churchill viewed Canada as a minor afterthought to the United States, visiting it much less often on his numerous lecture tours of North America. Perhaps oddly, he seemed much less at home in Canada than in the United States. After the Second World War, Churchill visited only Ottawa in Canada, on only two occasions (in 1952 and 1954), compared with six visits each to New York and Washington D.C., while he made his most famous post-war speech in Fulton, Missouri.

Churchill's main concern with the Empire appeared to centre clearly around the tropical realms and colonies, and how to maintain and increase British influence among its world-wide realms. His adamant opposition to Dominion status, or semi-Dominion status, for India in the 1930s has been discussed. Churchill framed his opposition to moves to Indian self-government to seem as if he had the welfare of ordinary Indians in mind, opposing British withdrawal in part because it would leave both the Untouchables, the Muslims, and other minorities at the mercy of a Hindu majority (which was perfectly true). But there also seems little doubt that he conceptualised British power and prestige in terms of areas painted pink on the world map (as did many others), and regarded the loss of India as a catastrophic blow to British prestige. Unlike many upper class English 'Arabists', Churchill had a generally low view of Muslims – which was one reason he was so warm towards Zionism, and hardly ever gave Black Africans a thought, but would certainly have regarded them as Stone Age savages, even if he phrased this view more diplomatically. Significantly, no British colonies gained independence during Churchill's post-war premiership in 1951–55. The first tropical colony to gain independence, Ghana, did so in 1957, two years after he retired. In 1953, the Central African Federation, composed of the wholly white-dominated governments of Northern Rhodesia, Southern Rhodesia, and Nyasaland (now Zambia, Zimbabwe, and Malawi) was established, and a year later suppressed the 'Mau Mau' rebellion in Kenya.

Churchill's relationships with the United States was also very ambiguous, despite his American background and his great reliance on it in peace and war. One notable feature of Churchill's connections with America is that he associated more frequently with Democrats than with Republicans. Democrats favoured Free Trade and were, on a range of issues (other than slavery and Reconstruction)

more 'progressive' than Republicans. Churchill's
closest American friend as a young man was the
Irish-born New York Democratic Congressman
Bourke Cockran. (Gilbert, *Churchill and America*,
pp.12–17; 46–49.) Cockran was one of the most
important influences on Churchill, although his
importance has not been recognised until recently.
In 1953 Adlai Stevenson asked Churchill who had
most influenced his public speaking techniques.
Remarkably, Churchill named Cockran, who 'taught
me how to use every note of the human voice like
an organ. He was my model.' (Cited in Gilbert,
Ibid., p.17.) Cochran's free trade views might
also have influenced Churchill at a critical time
in his career. From the First World War, as noted,
Churchill's closest American friend was probably
Bernard Baruch, a lifelong Democratic insider and
advisor (until he broke with Roosevelt in the later
1930s). In 1928 Baruch actually enlisted Churchill's
help in trying to elect Governor Al Smith, the
Democratic candidate for President, to the White
House. Churchill suggested the slogan 'Al for all all
for Al'. Baruch also suggested that Churchill ferret

out a compromising letter written many years earlier by Republican candidate Herbert Hoover, stating that under certain conditions he would become a British subject. Churchill refused to have anything to do with this proposal. (Gilbert, *Ibid.*, p.108.) When Churchill became Prime Minister in 1940, he of course had to deal on a daily basis with Democratic President Franklin Roosevelt, in an alliance which shaped the world. Churchill's virtual parting of the ways with Roosevelt over how to deal with Stalinist expansionism in the year before F.D.R.'s death is, of course, well known, although prior to that time relations between the two were cordial. Churchill also worked well with Roosevelt's successor Harry Truman, whose firmness towards Stalin he welcomed. In contrast, Churchill was privately alarmed at the election of Dwight Eisenhower as President in 1952, fearing it would increase the prospect of war. (Gilbert, *Ibid.*, p.414.) On an American visit in January 1953, Churchill, according to John Colville, privately had 'some very harsh things to say about the Republican Party in general and [newly appointed Secretary of

State John Foster] Dulles in particular … [whom] he disliked and distrusted.' (Cited in Gilbert, *Ibid.*, p.416.) Churchill's English Toryism thus did not make him especially warm towards American conservatives, unlike (say) Margaret Thatcher and Ronald Reagan a generation later. On the contrary, Churchill's progressive views, in the fore in his British career between about 1903 and 1922, were the lens with which he viewed American politics.

Churchill's belief in the hegemony of the 'English-speaking peoples' dates from no later than March 1918, when he wrote a Cabinet Minute claiming that 'the intermingling of British and American units on the field of battle and their endurance of losses and suffering together may exert an immeasurable effect upon the future destiny of the English-speaking peoples, and will afford us perhaps the only guarantee of safety if Germany emerges stronger from the War than she entered it.' (Cited in Gilbert, *Ibid.*, p.73.) This statement was made at the darkest hour of the War for Britain, when Germany had knocked Russia out of the conflict and appeared ready to win. It was at this time that Sir Douglas Haig issued his famous memorandum stating that Britain had 'its back to the wall'. Churchill was already envisioning America as the saviour of Britain in the long run. Hopes for the unity of the English-speaking peoples as the source of liberal political hegemony in the twentieth century were commonplace – they can be found, for instance, throughout Arthur Conan Doyle's Sherlock Holmes stories – but Churchill was possibly the only British politician of the front rank who actually believed in this concept and took it seriously. Churchill began to write his *History of the English-Speaking Peoples*, his famous multi-volume work, in December *1932*, for which he was offered an advance of £20,000 (around £1 million today). (Jenkins, *Churchill, op.cit.*, p.448.) It was not completed – Churchill was otherwise occupied – until 1957, but it seems clear that Churchill's belief in the historical unity and destiny of the English-speaking peoples long predated the Second World War. Churchill also visited the United States many times on lecture tours before 1939, and was probably the best-known

British politician in the United States even before he became Prime Minister. As is well-known, Churchill was almost killed in an automobile accident in New York in December 1931 when, unused to right-hand driving, he got out on the 'wrong side' of a taxi. In 1900, in Boston, Massachusetts, he was introduced to the 'other' Winston Churchill, the American writer who wrote a famous novel of the American Civil War, *The Crisis*, with whom for many years he was confused. The English Churchill allegedly told his American counterpart, 'Why don't you go into politics? I mean to be Prime Minister of England – it would be a great lark if you were President of the United States.' (Cited in Gilbert, *Churchill in America, op.cit.*, pp.39–40.)

All of this shows that Churchill was uniquely – and the term uniquely must be stressed – prepared to head the kind of war effort which Britain *had* to fight in 1940–41 and afterwards. By 1940, Churchill put his trust entirely in then-neutral America coming to the assistance of Britain, fighting alone, and eventually joining in the war as a super-power of incalculable strength. Without Churchill's faith in the Anglo-American alliance, it seems arguably that he would have advocated fighting on alone after the fall of France. Arguably any other possible British Prime Minister, especially Lord Halifax, would have attempted to make a deal with Hitler, one which Hitler repeatedly emphasised was on offer. It is difficult to think of any other major British politician of the time who was committed to an Anglo-American alliance to the same extent as Churchill, and most British Tories steered clear of it entirely. Neville Chamberlain, for instance, studiously excluded Franklin Roosevelt from any real role in negotiating European diplomacy. Chamberlain never met Roosevelt and certainly seldom if ever visited the United States or had any dealings with it. Churchill's pro-Americanism also made it far easier for him, out of necessity, to surrender many of Britain's overseas economic interests to America in lend-lease, and to allow American military leadership to dominate the joint war effort, with the previously-unknown Dwight Eisenhower being appointed Commander-in-Chief.

In recent years many right-wing historians such as John Charmley have criticised these preferences of Churchill's, as having sacrificed the British Empire for little in return. At the time and, to most since, they seemed inevitable choices. But only Winston Churchill could effortlessly make them. Churchill's stance on many controversial issues of his day were, with surprising regularity, both unusual and unexpected. But they always reflected his profound ability to reach the heart of any matter in dispute. Sometimes they were wrong, but they always bore the stamp of his genius.

CHURCHILL – ANOMALIES OF GREATNESS – BIBLIOGRAPHY

Addison, Paul, *Churchill on the Home Front, 1900–1955* (London, 1993)

Blake, Robert and Lewis, William Roger, eds., *Churchill* (Oxford, 1996)

Caputi, Robert J., *Neville Chamberlain and Appeasement* (Cranbury, N.J., 2000)

Churchill, Randolph S., *Winston S. Churchill: Volume II – The Young Statesman* (London, 1967)

Churchill, Winston S., "Zionism Versus Bolshevism: A Struggle for the Soul of the Jewish People," *Illustrated Sunday Herald*, 8 February 1920

Clodfelter, Micheal (sic), *Warfare and Armed Conflict: A Statistical Reference to Casualty and Other Figures, 1500–2000* (Jefferson, N.C., 2002)

Cohen, Michael J., *Churchill and the Jews* (London, 1985)

Croft, Lord [Henry Page Croft] *My Life of Strife* (London, n.d. [1947])

Foster, R.F., *Lord Randolph Churchill: A Political Life* (Oxford, 1981)

Gilbert, Martin, *Churchill and America* (London, 2005)

Gilbert, Martin, *Churchill and the Jews* (London, 2007)

Gilbert, Martin, *Winston S. Churchill, Volume 5, 1922–1939* (London, 1976)

Gilbert, Martin, *Winston Churchill: The Wilderness Years* (London, 1981)

Gilbert, Martin, *Winston S. Churchill: Part Four, Documents* (three volumes, London, 1977)

Grayson, Richard S., "Leo Amery's Imperialist

Alternatives to Appeasement in the 1930s, *Twentieth Century British History*, Vol. 17, part 4 (2007), pp. 489–515

Jay, Richard, *Joseph Chamberlain: A Political Study* (Oxford, 1981)

Jenkins, Roy, *Asquith* (London, 1967)

Jenkins, Roy, *Churchill* (London, 2001)

Marrison, Andrew, *British Business and Protection, 1903–1932* (Oxford, 1996)

Parker, R.A.C., *Churchill and Appeasement* London, 2000)

Rempel, Richard A., *Unionists Divided: Arthur Balfour, Joseph Chamberlain and the Unionist Free Traders* (Newton Abbot, 1972)

Rhodes James, Robert, ed., *Winston S. Churchill – His Complete Speeches, 1897–1963, Volume I: 1897–1908* (new York, 1974)

Rhodes James, Robert, ed., *Winston S. Churchill – His Complete Speeches, 1897–1963, Volume III, 1914–1922* (New York, 1974)

Rubinstein, William D., *The Myth of Rescue: Why the Democracies Could Not Have Saved More Jews From the Nazis* (London, 1997)

CHURCHILL –
ANOMALIES OF
GREATNESS –
INDEX

Addison, Christopher 76
Aitken Max, Lord
  Beaverbrook 11, 17,
  131
Amery, Leopold 9–10, 97,
  111
Appeasement, Supporters
  of 101–102
Asquith, H.H. 12,18,76
Attlee, Clement 125–6

Balance of Power, Germany
  and 86–91, 94–96
Baldwin, Stanley 17, 45, 46,
  80, 84, 97
Baruch, Bernard 107–9,
  136
Belloc, Hilaire 113–4
Bevin, Ernest 125–6
Bolshevism, Churchill and
  53–77

Bonar Law, Andrew 17, 21, 131

Boothby, Robert 85, 109

Bracken, Brendan 85, 109

British Empire, Churchill and 129–142

Carson, Sir Edward 56

Chamberlain, Joseph 2, 6–8, 34–35, 42, 131

Charmley, John 142

Churchill, Lord Randolph 24–5, 26, 113

Churchill, Winston (novelist) 140

Cockran, Bourke 23, 40, 136

Curzon, Lord 22, 131

Dulles, John Foster 138

Eisenhower, Dwight 137

Gandhi, Mohandas 83

Gilbert, Sir Martin 111 et al.

Halifax, Lord 83, 141

Hitler, Adolf 74, 94–5,

98–100, 119

Hoare, Sir Samuel 81, 84

Holocaust and the Allies 120–3

India, self-government 80–1

Irish Home Rule 55–56

Jerome, Jenny 25, 107

Jews, Churchill and the 105–127

Lenin, Vladimir 60, 67

Lindemann, Frederick 85, 109–110

Lloyd, Lord 80

Lloyd George, David 46, 47, 50, 55, 72 76, 83

Macdonald, Ramsay 45, 46, 50, 81–2, 84

Maisky, Ivan 76

Maxse, Leo 16–7

Moyne, Lord 110, 125

Namier, Sir Lewis 115

Nazis, Churchill and the 79–103

Northumberland, Duke of 57

Page Croft, Henry 10, 17, 57, 84
Palestine Mandate 115–6

Reeves, Emery 110–1
Reith, Sir John 81
Roosevelt, Franklin D. 137, 141

Sassoon, Sir Philip 109

Simon, Sir John 75, 84
Stalin, Joseph 92–3

Tariff Reform, Churchill and 1–52
Trotsky, Leon 60, 67
Truman, Harry 137

United States, Churchill and 39–40, 129–42

Weizmann, Chaim 110, 114–5, 124

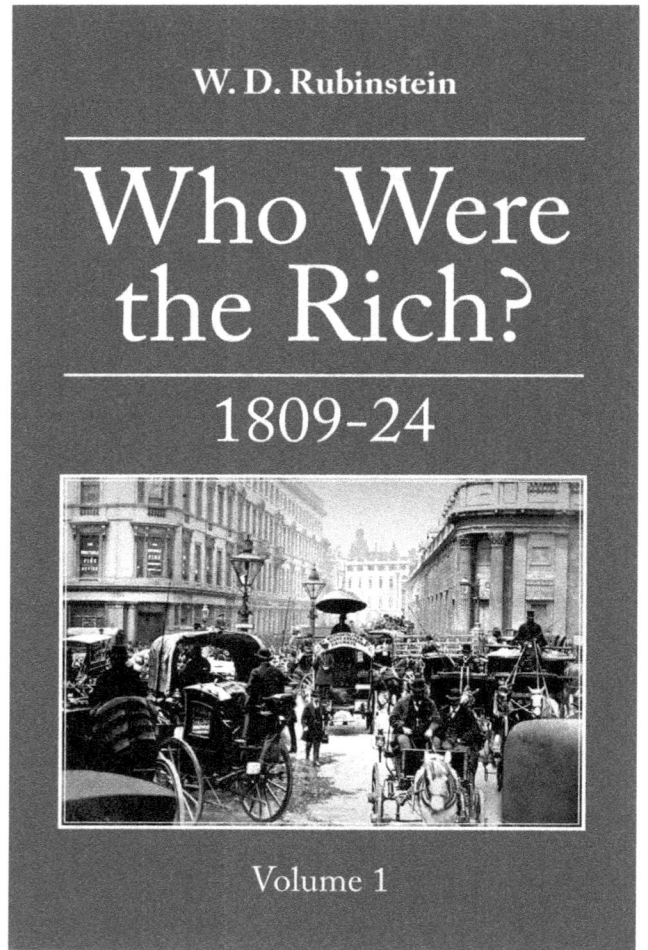

W. D. Rubinstein

Who Were the Rich?

1809-24

Volume 1

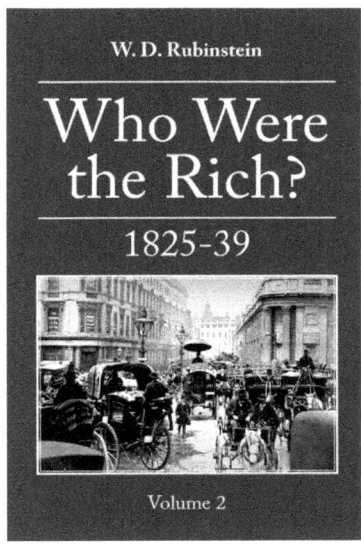

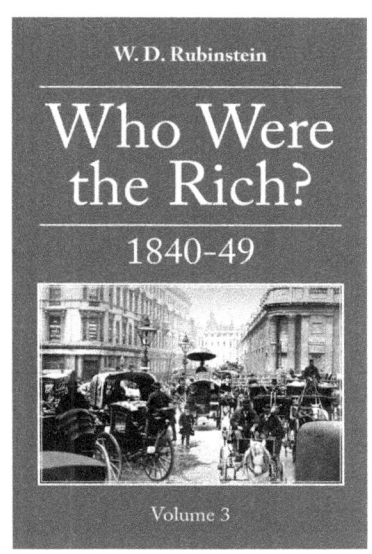

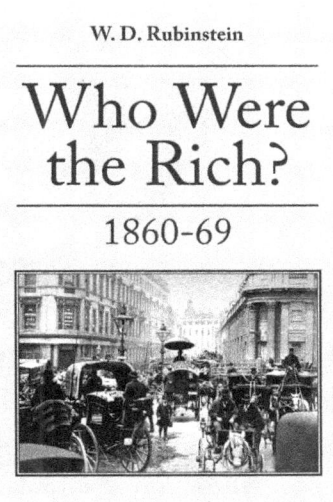

151

UNSOLVED
HISTORICAL
MYSTERIES

ANSWERS TO OUTSTANDING
HISTORICAL PUZZLES

W.D. Rubinstein

Elites and the Wealthy in
Modern British History

Essays in Social and Economic History

W.D. Rubinstein

NEW EXTENDED
EDITION

MEN OF
PROPERTY

THE VERY WEALTHY IN BRITAIN SINCE
THE INDUSTRIAL REVOLUTION

W.D. Rubinstein

NEW UPDATED EDITION

ALSO PUBLISHED BY EER

BEYOND THE DREAMS OF AVARICE

The Very Wealthy in Modern Britain

William D. Rubinstein

CPSIA information can be obtained
at www.ICGtesting.com
Printed in the USA
BVHW091358291120
594199BV00004B/15